*Back Lane Wineries*
*of*
# NAPA

# BACK LANE
## WINERIES OF
# NAPA

# TILAR MAZZEO

THE LITTLE BOOKROOM ✦ NEW YORK

©2010 The Little Bookroom

Text ©2010 Tilar J. Mazzeo

Photos (unless noted below) ©2010 Paul Hawley

Design: Jessica Hische / Louise Fili Ltd

Library of Congress Cataloging-in-Publication Data

Mazzeo, Tilar J.

Back-lane wineries of Napa / by Tilar J. Mazzeo; photographs by Paul Hawley.

p. cm.

Includes index.

ISBN 978-1-892145-83-3 (alk. paper)

1. Wine tasting—California—Napa Valley--Guidebooks. 2. Wineries—California—
Napa Valley—Guidebooks. 3. Napa Valley (Calif.)—Guidebooks. I. Title.

TP548.5.A5M396 2010

641.2'20979419—dc22

2009022775

Published by The Little Bookroom

435 Hudson Street, 3rd floor · New York NY 10014

editorial@littlebookroom.com · www.littlebookroom.com

Printed in China

Photo Credits:

page 125, 126 (bottom): © Ladera Vineyards.

page 148: © Robert Keenan Winery.

pages 197, 198-199, 200: © Ehlers Estate.

page 205: © Stony Hill Vineyard.

pages 216, 218: © Keever Vineyards.

# TABLE of CONTENTS

# INTRODUCTION

**T**HE REPUTATION OF THE NAPA VALLEY IS THE STUFF OF LEGEND, AND THE MAKING OF THE CALIFORNIA WINE country is a story with enough drama and intrigue to support more than a handful of best-selling accounts of its rise to international prominence. Since the famous face-off in the 1976 so-called "Judgment of Paris"—where Napa Valley chardonnay and cabernet sauvignon wines beat out renowned French competitors in blind tests—there has been no doubt that this relatively small corner of the wine world has garnered a big reputation. Consider, after all, that the Napa Valley produces less than five percent of the total wine production in the state of California. Or that it has fewer than 50,000 acres planted to vineyards. Bordeaux has more than five times that amount, and yet, devoted aficionados of Napa Valley wines will argue that their reputations are not all that different.

The result of all this celebrity and acclaim is more than just great wines. It also means tourism. Each year, more than five million visitors travel to the Napa Valley wine country from around the world, making it the second-largest tourist destination in the state after Disneyland. Most of these visitors travel along what the locals simply call the loop—the well-trodden tasting route that takes eager enthusiasts up the Silverado Trail and back down the St. Helena Highway (or vice versa), past some of America's most famous and most familiar wineries. Along the way, there are picturesque fields of blazing mustard blooms, ready gourmet pleasures, and a little taste of the good life, Napa style.

If what you want is a weekend (or more) of incomparable luxury, you'll have no trouble finding it here in the wine country, and you won't need a travel guide if what you want to do is visit the celebrated commercial wineries of the Napa Valley. It's hard to miss them. Many tasting rooms are slick retail operations run by corporate managers living somewhere a long way from Napa, offering wines that you can buy just as readily (and often less expensively) on the shelves of your local grocery store, and big signs along the highway will show you the way. Often, these are beautiful places, and I am not recommending that you pass them by entirely. A part of the California wine tasting experience is sitting on marbled Italianate terraces overlooking acres of perfectly pruned vineyards, basking in the warm sun and the intense loveliness of it all.

But for some, as exquisite as it all is, there is also a whispered complaint. To certain sensibilities, it's just possible that this aspect of Napa is a bit more like Disneyland than anyone would like. The largest corporate wineries crank out more than eight million cases of wine a year, and the hillsides are dotted with mansions that you can tell even from a distance are monstrously huge. It's all too easy to get the impression that Napa is big business by day and elite charity events by night—the kind of place where the idle super-rich, weighed down by all those diamonds, struggle to lift that $100 glass of hillside cabernet. And sometimes there is the perception that only heaven can help the poor novice who wanders off the beaten tourist track. At least there, lost in a crowd, you can slink away silently when the expert palates start in on some competitive and very expensive appreciation.

These are some of the enduring stereotypes of Napa—maybe even part of the marketing in some corners of the valley. But nothing could be further from the heart and soul of this region. The other side of the wine country, and by far the larger side, is surprisingly genuine, low-key, and embracing, a place where enthusiastic amateurs are everyone's favorite people and where you can spend a long afternoon tromping the vineyards with a small proprietor who is only too happy to share with you his or her little piece of paradise for a remarkably modest tasting fee—and sometimes without charging at all. Out there in the fields or up in the tasting room, you'll hear time and time again the story of how one winemaker or another came to this verdant valley, fell in love with it, and found the course of life irrevocably altered. Everywhere in Napa there are people of passion, who have made their life's work crafting a beautiful wine.

And, here in the wine country, there are also more than a few families who have farmed these ranches for decades and can still remember a time when most of this valley was planted not to grapes but to fruit orchards. These are folks with deep community ties and pioneering histories—and part of what they helped to pioneer was that special way of life in the wine country that still has the power to enchant so many of those who come to visit.

But it's only along the back lanes that you'll get to hear these kinds of stories, and, because many of these wines aren't widely distributed, it's also only along the back lanes that you'll get a chance to try them. They are, as often as not, world-class wines that locals and industry insiders revere but that few consumers will ever encounter in a wine shop. Without the pressures of large-scale commercialization, these are also the cellars where old varietals can be preserved or new experiments in shaping the future of oenology can be put to the test.

These small outfits won't have big advertising budgets or well-posted tasting rooms along the major thoroughfares—and they don't want them, either. So the trouble for a newcomer to the Napa Valley is where to start looking. This is a guide to those back lane wineries of Napa, places where you can find excellent handcrafted wines made by on-site proprietors, often with only a local or regional distribution and with a limited case production. The vast majority of the wineries included in this book make fewer than 10,000 cases of wine a year, and the smallest produce only a hundred or so. The largest make fewer than 35,000 cases, and, in a county where some of the big commercial operations churn out millions of cases of wine a year, this is still a small operation. Off the beaten path there are few marble terraces or stucco palaces, but often these wineries are in the midst of striking beauty—overlooking a hundred acres of a wildlife preserve far above the fog-lined valley floor, on the edge of an ancient redwood forest, or simply tucked along a rural side road in the middle of open fields, where the proprietors are happy to watch you settle down for a picnic with a bottle or two of wine.

Best of all, in my mind, these are places where wine tasting gets down to earth. Here, no one needs to show off how developed his or her palate is, and the winemakers welcome questions, from beginners and experts alike. Often, you will also find that these are the wineries where sustainable and organic viticulture is being pioneered. Above all, these are wines that are likely to be a new experience, with names that you won't find in big retail outlets back home. Amid the back lane wineries of Napa, you can still make secret discoveries.

〜〜〜

T HE NAPA VALLEY WINE-GROWING REGION, ONE OF THE
WORLD'S MOST RECOGNIZABLE APPELLATIONS IN ITS OWN
right, encompasses more than a dozen sub-appellations
(currently fourteen, but a fifteenth, Calistoga, is pending),
each with a particular microclimate and with particular grape
varietals that thrive in the region, and often the wines are remarkably
distinct. Visitors are often surprised to discover that a relatively small
area can produce wines of such diversity.

This diversity is the result of the area's geological history, which has
created a long, narrow valley, running some thirty-odd miles between
two steep mountain ranges along the ancient contours of the Napa River, from the San Pablo Bay in the south to as far north as Calistoga, at the
foot of Mount St. Helena. The Vacas Mountains rise up above the valley
floor to the east, and they are home to some of the region's most famous
hillside vineyards, including the celebrated Howell Mountain sub-appellation. To the west are the Mayacamas, which divide Napa County
from nearby Sonoma County, and where highly regarded new vineyards
are being developed.

Two main roads run the length of the valley floor. On the western side
of the valley is Highway 29, which is also known as the St. Helena Highway, and this is the region's main tasting route. It takes visitors through
the area's small towns, where you will find restaurants, hotels, and, of
course, tasting rooms. On the eastern side of the valley is Highway 121,
which, when it runs through the wine country, is known as the Silverado
Trail—or to locals simply as "the trail"—a more rural and scenic road
that passes acres of vineyards and is dotted with dozens of premium

wineries. Directions are given from one or both of these routes, and your best bet for navigating the region is to pick up one of the free maps available at almost any tasting room or hotel.

If Highway 29 and the Silverado Trail may be said to run roughly parallel to each other, you'll also want to know that they are connected at various points by a series of crossroads, beginning with Trancas Street to the south, in the town of Napa, and, progressing northward, Oak Knoll Avenue, Yountville Cross Road, Oakville Cross Road, Highway 128 at Rutherford Road, Zinfandel Lane, Deer Park Road, Lodi Lane, Bale Lane, Larkmead Lane, and Highway 29 at Lincoln Avenue, in the town of Calistoga. Those are your best bets for getting from one side of the valley to the other, and, though the locals won't thank me for mentioning it, it's handy to know that, when the traffic on the St. Helena Highway is too hopelessly congested to bear, things are often much quicker just a bit to the east.

Although the region is world famous for its wines, much of the valley remains uncultivated, and as a result the Napa Valley American Viticultural Area—or AVA—is spread out over a relatively large area. Because it can easily take more than an hour of steady driving to get across the region, the best way to plan a day of wine tasting is to focus on a couple of sub-appellations, taking time for a leisurely gourmet lunch and some sightseeing along the way. (And if you are visiting up in the mountains or in the eastern valleys, keep in mind that the only dependable options for either gasoline or lunch are in Napa or along the St. Helena Highway.)

To understand AVA classifications in the Napa Valley, it's important to remember that Napa Valley is its own AVA. Within that larger wine-growing region there are also more than a dozen distinct sub-appellations, areas characterized by especially distinct growing conditions and microclimates, including Howell Mountain, Chiles Valley District, Atlas

Peak, Spring Mountain District, Mount Veeder, Los Carneros, Oak Knoll District of Napa Valley, Stag's Leap, Yountville, Oakville, Wild Horse Valley, Rutherford, St. Helena, Diamond Mountain, and Calistoga (approval pending). Some of the smaller and more remote areas—places like Atlas Peak, Wild Horse Valley, Mount Veeder, and Diamond Mountain District AVA—have very limited opportunities for visits, and many of the wineries in these areas maintain tasting rooms down on the valley floor. For this reason, these wineries can be found mixed in among the different sections of this book.

While understanding the nuances of appellations is important to appreciating the wines from the Napa Valley, this guide is arranged loosely by route rather than strictly by classification, with an eye toward helping you plan a convenient tasting itinerary that might take in a couple of different wine-growing areas. It's a chance in the course of a day (or more) to experience just how different one growing region can be from the next—even when the distance is only a matter of miles or minutes. At the end of each section are suggestions for nearby restaurants or local attractions that you can work in spontaneously.

The book is divided into nine different tasting areas:

- **DOWNTOWN NAPA** and Environs includes wineries and tasting rooms conveniently clustered around the city of Napa, where you'll also find outdoor markets, some of the valley's best evening entertainment, and good casual dining options.

- **SILVERADO TRAIL** covers wineries along this famous tasting route on the eastern side of the Napa Valley and includes the acclaimed Stag's Leap and Oak Knoll Districts.

- **CALISTOGA** and Environs includes the tasting rooms conveniently clustered along the north end of the Silverado Trail and the St. Helena Highway within easy striking distance of the city of Calistoga, renowned for its mineral baths and home to some excellent casual dining opportunities.

- **HOWELL MOUNTAIN** AVA takes in the sometimes remote and always lovely Howell Mountain wineries that are located in the foothills on the eastern side of the Napa Valley.

- **SPRING MOUNTAIN DISTRICT** takes in the equally remote and equally beautiful mountain wineries that are located in the foothills on the western side of the Napa Valley.

- **DOWNTOWN ST. HELENA** and Environs covers wineries in the area immediately surrounding the picturesque town of St. Helena, home to some of the region's most charming small shops and mouthwatering bistros. This section includes wineries that are producing primarily in the St. Helena AVA.

- **ST. HELENA HIGHWAY** encompasses the small family tasting rooms tucked among the commercial giants along Highway 29 and includes tasting-room options in the Rutherford, Oakville, and Yountville AVAs. Wine aficionados will know that the town of Yountville is also deservedly famous for its world-class dining options.

- **EASTERN VALLEYS** covers the smaller and more remote valleys tucked into the eastern foothills of the Napa Valley, including the Chiles Valley District and the Pope Valley AVA.

- **LOS CARNEROS** and Environs South of Napa includes the cooler-climate growing region of the Carneros AVA and some of the off the beaten path wineries located south of the city of Napa.

Within all regions, you can also find wines produced within the more general—and immediately recognizable—Napa Valley AVA.

All the wineries listed in this book are open to visitors, and wine-tasting hours throughout the county are generally from 10AM to 4:30PM daily, although some wineries have longer or shorter hours, and it is always a good idea to call ahead to confirm opening times, especially early in the week (Monday and Tuesday particularly). Groups larger than six people should always call ahead to be sure the winemakers can accommodate them.

Many of the best small wineries are open by appointment only. You should not feel the least bit shy about making the call. If a winemaker requires advance notice, it just means that he or she wants to be sure the tasting room is staffed that afternoon, and it is usually a sign that the person behind the bar will be the same person who goes out pruning the vines other days of the week. (And, due to local zoning legislation and efforts to preserve the rural agricultural charm of the area, the trend is moving very strongly in the direction of "by appointment only.") Often these winemaker tours are exceptional educational experiences and a rare opportunity to get an inside perspective on the craft of winemaking. Generally, it's a good idea to call at least a week in advance to set up appointments, and, in the busy summer months, appointments several weeks in advance are strongly recommended. But should you find yourself in the wine country unexpectedly, there's absolutely no harm in making a spur-of-the-moment call. Often, the winemakers are able to welcome even last-minute visitors.

When you are planning your trip, keep in mind that weekends are the busiest time for wine tasting, especially at the commercial wineries, and in the summer months you will often have to jostle for a place at the tasting bar. A busy Saturday is the perfect time to head off the beaten path and visit some of the back lane wineries. Locals prefer to go wine tasting on Thursdays and Friday mornings, when most places are open and gearing up for the weekend. If you are planning to visit in late-August or September, plan with particular care: the harvest—known in the California wine country simply as "the crush"—takes place around then, and the tasting room hours can be limited, but there are often opportunities to participate in other special events and harvest suppers during what can be one of the most festive times of the winemaking year.

And what will all this cost? Many tasting rooms (and nearly all the commercial ones) charge modest tasting fees, ranging from ten to fifteen dollars for a "flight" of wines—usually a small taste of about a half-dozen different wines. It generally costs a bit more to taste the more expensive and acclaimed "reserve" wines ($25 and up is common), and the best of those experiences are sit-down private appointments with a winemaker that can last an hour or more. Generally, it's a good idea to budget an hour and a half for each visit, unless a winemaker specifies otherwise. If you want to visit several wineries, no one will mind in the least if you ask to share a flight with your tasting companions, and in many cases the cost of your tasting fees will be waived if you buy even a single bottle of wine.

In some places, especially in the smaller back-road wineries, there will be no charge for tasting and no charge even for the winemaker tours, and there is never any obligation to buy wine. But winemaking is an expensive business and for many of these small proprietors this is a labor of love. Buying someone's wine after you've enjoyed it is the best compliment, and my own rule of thumb for wine tasting etiquette is that, if there is no charge for the tasting, the polite thing to do is buy a bottle or two. When there is a charge for the tasting, I only buy the wines I know I will enjoy. But because tasting fees are so often waived with a purchase, it never makes any sense to me not to buy a bottle at each winery.

Napa County is justly famous for its restaurants, which include some of the finest dining experiences anywhere—and often at equally rarefied prices. But it's also possible to eat sumptuously here in the wine country on a budget, and the streets of small towns like Yountville, St. Helena, and Calistoga are filled with excellent bistros, where the industry insiders gather after the tasting rooms close to enjoy a good meal and small-production wines.

In the summer, there are local farmers markets up and down Highway 29, and the Friday evening Chef's Market in downtown Napa, where you can shop for regional delicacies and listen to live music, has been part of the city's gourmet renaissance in recent years. The local grocery stores and specialty shops are stocked with an astonishing variety of artisanal meats, cheeses, and produce, where you can find all the fixings for an impromptu vineyard picnic.

The restaurant recommendations in this guide highlight places where you are welcome to enjoy your most recent discovery for a modest corkage fee. These are invariably also places that have excellent local wine lists, where perhaps new discoveries await. After all, there's no reason that experiencing the best of Napa's back lane wineries has to end just because it's mealtime. In many cases I suggest unique small-lot wines that are on the wine lists at my favorite places—wines made by people whose production is so limited that there are no tasting rooms at all. These are highly acclaimed wines that you wouldn't otherwise be able to sample, although you can order them directly from the winemakers if you're looking to add something special to your cellars. And, above all of course, in a part of the world where fine dining is a serious undertaking, these are restaurants where you can settle in for a relaxed and delicious long afternoon lunch or where you can celebrate that special occasion with a bottle of something that you'll never find back home.

# WINE TASTING ESSENTIALS

**E**VEN SOPHISTICATED WINE AFICIONADOS SOMETIMES FIND THEMSELVES WONDERING WHAT THE "RIGHT" WAY TO TASTE wine is, and, as you anticipate sitting down face-to-face with a winemaker, it's easy to start worrying about whether you'll pass the test. There's no need: in the wine country, the friendliest welcome of all is reserved for passionate amateurs. And you're not the only one who gets the giggles when that gentleman at the far end of the tasting bar starts throwing around wildly improbable adjectives.

However, if you want to refresh yourself on the basics before embarking on your wine tasting adventures, it's easily done. For starters, hold the wine glass by the stem. Cupping it in your hands and leaving greasy fingerprints not only looks decidedly unglamorous, but will also warm the wine, changing its aromas. The experts will tell you that "tasting" wine is largely about aroma. We can only experience six different tastes, and nature's way around the limited range of our taste buds is to marry those perceptions to the thousand or more different smells that we can detect, creating seemingly endless delights for the gourmet. This is the whole point of swirling and sniffing your wine.

When you are handed a glass—and your tasting typically will progress from the lightest wine to the most intense wine in the flight—begin by gently tilting it to look at the clarity and colors. Unless you're an expert, the conclusion you'll probably reach is that it looks delicious, but a trained eye will be looking to assess alcohol content, barrel aging, and structural components. Then, give the glass a swirl. Many of us accomplish this most gracefully by keeping the glass on the table and making a few quick circles, but if you're the daring sort there's always the risk of a mid air execution to perfect as the afternoon wears on. The point is that the movement begins to open the bouquet of the wine. You are supposed to start with a gentle sniff with your nose above the glass, then move on to a deeper sniff with your nose right down there in the stemware. As a wine drinker and not a contest judge, what you're looking for is a sensory experience that will help you pick out the different aromas that are going to shape how this wine is going to taste for you.

The next step—finally—is to take a sip of wine. But remember that the taste buds are in your mouth and not down your gullet. So roll the wine around in your mouth for a few moments, making sure it reaches the different parts of your tongue, where the distinct tastes and textures are experienced. Before you swallow, you can also try pulling a little air over your teeth and breathing in through your nose to aspirate the wine and intensify the experience of the aroma.

There is also a technique where you can attempt to slurp the wine silently and draw the vapors into your sinuses, usually effected by placing your tongue on the outside of the glass as you drink and inhaling simultaneously. If you do it right, the result is what the experts call retro-olfaction—a concentrated explosion of aroma that takes the information your brain needs to process smell more directly to your neurological receptors—but if you do it wrong, you'll end up sputtering wine rather dramatically. It might be wise to practice at home first, or if you find yourself wine tasting without an audience, ask one of the winemakers to show you how it's done.

You may also see some fellow tasters spit the wine out without swallowing in the course of your tasting adventures. That's perfectly acceptable, and it's the reason tasting rooms all have those dump buckets on the counter. All those little sips of wine add up quickly, after all.

If you're lucky enough to be invited to a barrel tasting, spitting is *de rigueur*. These are wines still in the making, and no one expects them to be of a finished, drinkable quality. Barrel tasting is an exceptional opportunity to learn about how the structure and aromas of a wine develop over time. Winemakers are happy to explain what is happening with a wine at any given moment, and learning how to judge how a wine evolves is an essential element of connoisseurship.

# SHIPPING WINES HOME

---

**F**OR MANY VISITORS TO NAPA, THE TROUBLE IS FINDING WAYS TO GET ALL THESE WONDERFUL WINES HOME. AND when you have been touring the back lane wineries, discovering small-production, handcrafted wines that won't be available at home, the question takes on a particular urgency. Most of the wineries in this book distribute their wines only through their tasting-room sales, and this is part of what makes discovering them so satisfying.

Depending on where you live, there are several excellent options for getting your purchases back to your home cellar. Many wineries will ship your purchases home to you directly, provided your state allows this. The costs are generally prohibitive for a single bottle of wine, but for several it is quite reasonable. For purchases of a case or more, ask whether there is flexibility in their wine club program. The discounts are significant if you are a member, and generally your only commitment is agreeing to purchase a case of wine over the course of the year. Often, the wineries want to ship the wines to you quarterly, but, when I wanted to get a few cases to my summer place in New England, I never had any trouble persuading local winemakers to send me the entire annual allotment at once, at a significant savings in the shipping.

You can also ship the wines home directly through commercial freight companies, and there are also a number of smaller shops that specialize in helping visitors to the wine country get their precious cargo safely to its destination. These shops often supply specially designed case-sized wine shippers for a minimal fee, and, if you live in a state where wineries are prohibited from mailing wines directly to consumers, this may be your best option for sending a case or two home ahead of you. The price for shipping a case, without insurance, to the East Coast generally runs around $80, with prices less for shorter distances. At the end of this book, I list some shops that I have found particularly easy to work with.

Another option is to send the wine as checked luggage, and this is frankly my favorite. I have done it for years and only very rarely has a bottle broken *en route*. A sturdy cardboard box, marked fragile, can get an entire case of wine across the country with minimal hassle, provided you understand the airline policies and any unusual state sales-tax regulations (available from your local bureau of taxation). Most wineries will happily give you a regular packing box, and some of the wineries have started selling extra-sturdy boxes specifically designed for sending wines this way. You can also purchase a "wine lover's suitcase" from catalog suppliers before your trip and rest easy knowing that your only worry is finding favorite bottles to fill it up.

And for those extra special, high-end purchases destined for the cellars of the serious collector, there are always third-party shippers who specialize in sending wines anywhere you need them to go. On page 266, I list my favorite ones, or you can ask at any premium winery for recommendations.

Even if you take nothing home with you as a souvenir for your cellar, the back lane wineries of Napa are an experience few visitors ever forget. Off the beaten path and along the back roads, amid oak trees and mustard blooms, the experience of wine tasting is immediate and personal. May your journey and discoveries be as individual as your palate, and welcome to the heart of the Napa Valley.

# DOWNTOWN NAPA

The first Native American inhabitants of this region were the Wappo, who named the valley the "land of plenty"—or Napa. Those who have since settled in this magical corner of the world have been struck by the same sense of its special bounty. The wine country to the north of San Francisco was renowned in the 1850s and 1860s for its gold and silver, which led to some of California's most fabled mining rushes and to the establishment of many of the small towns that tourists enjoy today.

During the latter years of the nineteenth century and throughout the twentieth century, the Napa Valley was famous for its fruit production—part of which already included, by the 1870s, the region's acclaimed vineyards. But it wasn't until the 1970s that Napa became America's most recognizable wine country. While the county of Napa and the wines made here have international recognition, visitors are often less familiar with the city of Napa, which is the gateway to the tasting trail. But in your travels, it's worth a stop. In recent years, the city has been undergoing an urban renaissance, and today it is a vibrant small community with some of the area's best local produce, small family restaurants, and engaging evening entertainment. During the warm summer evenings, families (and visitors) stroll the streets, taking in some of the live music or making impromptu meals in the al fresco markets. Best of all, of course, there are an increasing number of small tasting rooms right in the heart of the city, where you can continue to make some discoveries after hours.

# OLABISI WINERY

974 Franklin Street ✦ Napa

Downtown Napa, between First and Second avenues

*Tel:* 707.257.7477 ✦ www.olabisiwines.com

Tasting daily 11AM *to* 6PM

**T**HIS INTIMATE TASTING ROOM IN DOWNTOWN NAPA IS CHIC AND COOL AND THE PERFECT PLACE TO STOP BY IN THOSE late afternoon hours, when the back lane wineries aren't making appointments but it's too early to sit down to a mouthwatering dinner with a bottle of your favorite new discovery.

The small winery run by Ted Osborne and Kim Wedlake is certainly worth a stop. Ted is a well-known winemaker here in the Napa Valley, having worked most recently for Storybook Mountain Winery and Piña Cellars. But, in his years in the industry, he's also worked around the world, crafting vintages in Australia, France, and, of course, here in California. For his Olabisi label, Ted makes some French-style chardonnay, an old-vine zinfandel, a syrah, and a petite sirah. The emphasis is on exploring complexity in a single site, working with a natural

style, and delivering a great value. "Killer wines at killer prices" (ranging from $30–45) is the motto here, Ted will tell you. The tasting fee is $10 for five wines, and don't be surprised if the guy pouring is the wine-maker himself. The name Olabisi, for those who are wondering, comes from an African girl's name meaning "joy multiplied."

# TRAHAN WINERY

974 Franklin Street ✦ Napa
Downtown Napa, between First and Second avenues
*Tel:* 707.257.7477 ✦ www.trahanwinery.com
Tasting daily 11AM to 6PM

SHARING A TASTING ROOM WITH OLABISI IS ALSO THE TRAHAN FAMILY WINERY, RUN BY CHUCK CUSTODIO, HIS wife Janna, and mother Liz. They released their first vintage in 2004 at Chuck and Janna's wedding—two hundred cases of a Napa Valley cabernet sauvignon. They now produce about a thousand cases of wine a year, and, if you're looking for a good story about how the Napa Valley and a passion for winemaking can change lives, Chuck has one. The way he tells it, he was working as a corporate type in high-tech manufacturing in the Bay area when it suddenly occurred to him that he needed to think about whether this was what he really wanted to be doing for the next thirty years.

The answer to that question was a resounding no, and so Chuck took one of those plunges that the wine country seems to inspire in people. On a weekend break in the valley, he found himself on the wine train, which rolls visitors through Napa County in old-fashioned luxury (707.253.2111, www.winetrain.com), and he realized that he had discovered his passion. Soon after, a small boutique winery hired him, and, for the next four years, Chuck worked for $12 an hour, commuting two hours each way between Calistoga and San Francisco, learning the craft and taking night courses in winemaking at the Napa Valley Community College.

The result of this dedication is Trahan Winery. Sourcing grapes from vineyards around Northern California and working with Ted Osborne as a consulting winemaker, Trahan produces almost a half-dozen different wines, including an acclaimed 100% petit verdot, a merlot, a cabernet sauvignon, some barrel-fermented chardonnay, and, recently, fewer than sixty cases of an excellent Carneros pinot noir. Wines range from $30–45, and the tasting fee is $10.

# CEJA VINEYARDS

1248 First Street ✦ Napa

Downtown Napa

*Tel:* 707.255.3954 ✦ www.cejavineyards.com

Tasting daily Noon to 6PM, closed Wednesday

WHILE THE MAIN TASTING ROOMS FOR THE CEJA FAMILY VINEYARDS ARE ON A BACK LANE OVER IN THE Carneros (see page 253), here at their Napa tasting salon, the pace is more urban, and you can stop in while enjoying the live music on Friday evenings in the summer. On Saturday nights, son Ariel offers complimentary salsa dancing lessons from 7:30 to 8:30 in the tasting salon, and a dance party—with Ceja wines by the glass—follows until 11PM (no cover). It's one of the hippest spots in the valley.

Of course, you can also taste the full range of Ceja wines (tasting fee $15). The family has something for every taste, ranging from Carneros chardonnay and pinot noir wines to a Napa Valley cabernet sauvignon and a botrytis white port-style dessert wine of chardonnay and sauvignon blanc. There is also a range of cooler-climate wines made from grapes sourced on the Sonoma Coast, and a syrah port (most wines from $22–55).

# FONTANELLA FAMILY WINERY

1721 Partrick Road ✦ Napa
Exit Highway 29 west on First Avenue *to*
Browns Valley Road, right *to* Partrick Road
*Tel:* 707.252.1017 ✦ www.fontanellawinery.com
Tasting daily 10AM *to* 4PM ✦ by appointment only

**T**HE FONTANELLA FAMILY WINERY IS NESTLED IN THE WESTERN HILLS OF NAPA, ON THE SOUTHERN TIP OF THE Mount Veeder appellation, and owners Jeff and Karen Fontanella confess that they might have been just a bit delirious when they first decided to build a winery on the property. The process of negotiating the land-use permits alone took the couple two years. Fortunately, Karen came to the wine business after a career practicing real estate law. Jeff, meanwhile, had built a reputation working as a winemaker at some of the valley's big names, including Opus One and Saddleback. It seemed like the perfect opportunity to live part of the wine-country dream.

Today, the Fontanella tasting room and winery, which opened to the public in the summer of 2008, is one of the county's charming

pastoral retreats. The tasting room looks out over a tranquil pond, and there are views of the hills in the distance. On cooler days, guests settle in around the fireplace, and in the summer months tasting takes place on the long back patio. The couple runs the tasting room, and Jeff, of course, is the winemaker, so this is an intimate and personal experience, where visitors get a chance to meet the people behind the wines and perhaps to make some new friends in the valley.

Currently Jeff and Karen make just three wines—a chardonnay, a zinfandel, and a cabernet sauvignon ($30–55)—and these are all small-lot wines, handcrafted from local fruit sources and, soon, from estate vineyards on their twenty-six-acre bit of paradise.

# CALDWELL VINEYARD

169 Kruezer Lane ✦ Napa

Silverado Trail (Highway 121) *to* Coombsville Road,

south on Fourth Avenue *to* Kruezer Lane

*Tel:* 707.255.1294 ✦ www.caldwellvineyard.com

Tasting by appointment only

FROM THE HILLTOP ESTATE AT CALDWELL VINEYARDS, THERE ARE VIEWS OF THE NAPA VALLEY IN BOTH DIRECTIONS. YOU can see as far as the Carneros if you look one way, and the peak of Mount St. Helena if you look the other. In the foreground, of course, there are vineyards—fifty-seven acres of them. When John Caldwell bought this property in the 1980s, his first idea was to subdivide and resell. Transforming this unique corner of the Napa Valley into an estate winery came later,

after he had fallen in love with this bit of earth.

These days the family—John and his wife Joy, along with his father Jack and wife Alma—produces around 3,500 cases a year on a ranch that John likes to joke doesn't have a naturally flat place on it. Caldwell Vineyards has built its reputation working with unusual clones, and the focus is on keeping the wines as purely expressive as possible. This means that winemaker Marbue Marke prefers traditional artisanal methods such as whole berry and barrel fermentation.

But there's a bit more to the Caldwell clonal story as well. Back in the 1970s, John smuggled some of these vines in from France in a story that's full of high drama and intrigue. You want to be sure to ask him for the story about how he ate—that's right, ate—the incriminating receipts some Canadian customs officers found in the trunk of his vehicle crossing the border. Or about how he hid the vines from the authorities by burying them under an old oak tree on the property. Eventually, realizing that the life of a smuggler was fraught with peril, John took up legal importing and became the first winemaker in the country to grow vines brought over from some of the world's most prestigious French vineyards.

Wine devotees will still appreciate the Caldwell clonal-variety collection. The vineyard also produces a small amount of its signature ultra-premium Napa Valley cabernet sauvignon and a cabernet and syrah blend (ranging from $65–150). There is an excellent proprietary red "Rocket Science" blend and well-priced rosé and chardonnay wines (around $20–50).

Private tasting appointments include a tour of the underground winery, a chance to take in the views, and time to sample the wines, which the family pairs with local cheeses and expert conversation. The $45 tasting fee is waived with purchase.

# ANCIEN WINES

4047 East Third Avenue ✦ Napa
Silverado Trail (Highway 121) to Coombsville Road,
north on Third Avenue to East Third Avenue
*Tel.* 707.255.3908 ✦ www.ancienwines.com
Tasting by appointment only

OWNED AND OPERATED BY KEN BERNARDS AND HIS WIFE TERESA, ANCIEN WINES SPECIALIZES IN MAKING HAND-crafted pinot noir, pinot gris, and chardonnay wines ($22–50), which Ken discovered a passion for in the 1980s when he was completing a chemistry degree at Oregon State University, in the heart of the Willamette Valley wine country.

Ancien is located east of the city of Napa, where few tourists ever come, on the site of the historic Haynes vineyards. The property has had working vineyards on it since 1885, when the Haynes family purchased it from Nathan Coombs, one of the first white settlers in the Napa Valley. The original vineyards were destroyed in the fires that spread after the great San Francisco earthquake of 1906, but, in 1966, Duncan and Pat Haynes replanted the property to pinot noir and chardonnay under the tutelage of Napa wine pioneer Louis Martini, Sr., making it one of the oldest pinot noir and chardonnay vineyards in California. Blocks of these early vines are still in production today.

The winemaker's tour includes a walk through the vineyards and, in the warmer months, a tasting under the oak trees, with views of Mount George and the foothills of the Vacas range. During the rainy months, you'll sample by candlelight in the barrel room at a small wooden table.

In addition to the wine produced from fruit grown here in the Haynes vineyards, Ken also sources pinot noir from other spots in the Carneros AVA, Sonoma County, the Willamette Valley, and the Santa Rita Hills.

Best of all, if you're looking to learn more about the wines that you are discovering here in the Napa Valley, the tasting experience at Ancien is one of the best educational opportunities in the county. The winery welcomes everyone from serious pinot noir collectors to new enthusiasts looking for a crash course in Wine 101. There's a chance to do barrel tasting and to learn firsthand how different barrels made at different cooperages affect the flavor of the wines. You'll learn about head-pruned vines and what makes an Alsatian-style pinot gris and how the afternoon breezes shape the microclimate. The hour-and-a-half tour and tasting is $40 per person, waived for members—new or old—of their wine club.

# FRAZIER FAMILY ESTATE WINERY

70 Rapp Lane ✦ Napa
Silverado Trail (Highway 121) to Hagen Road,
right onto First Avenue, left onto North Avenue,
left onto Second Avenue to Rapp Lane
*Tel.* 707.255.3444 extension 107 ✦ www.frazierwinery.com
Tasting by appointment only

**R**APP LANE IS A SMALL WINDING TRACK THAT LEADS TO THE LUPINE HILL VINEYARD, WHICH TAKES ITS NAME FROM THE wildflowers that cover the slopes of this hillside property to the east of Napa. The local legend tells that the Christian Brothers monks, who once lived in this part of the county and cultivated the vineyards here, planted these flowers, which long ago escaped their gardens. In the late spring, visitors of the Frazier Family Estate Winery drive through lanes awash in color.

When airline pilot Bill Frazier bought his first parcel of hillside property here in the early 1980s, it was the beginning of a dream that would end up capturing the imagination of his entire family. In 1990, he planted ten acres of vineyards, and the Frazier winery was established as a small operation, producing less than a thousand cases of wine a year. Since then, the winery has grown steadily, and today the estate produces around 3,500 cases a year from seventy-odd acres of land. Bill runs the winery with the help of several of his children, including son Jon, who is the vineyard manager, and daughter Kim, who manages marketing and operations. Her husband, Adam, manages the tasting room and sales.

The family produces a range of estate wines made with cabernet sauvignon, merlot, petit verdot, cabernet franc, and a small planting of chardonnay grapes. The flagship wine is the luscious Memento reserve cabernet, which they release along with merlot- and cabernet-based blends, the occasional petit verdot, chardonnay, and a port-style dessert wine (most wines from $40–80, reserve wines starting at $110).

The winery is a cave dug into this scenic hillside property, and tasting takes place in the so-called Marrakesh room—a cellar tasting room warmed with Moroccan carpets, soft leather chairs, and candlelight. Here, around a long oak table, one of the members of the family will lead you through a sensory appreciation of the wines and take you on a tour of the cellars, where barrel tasting is offered throughout the year. The fee for the tasting and tour is $30, waived with purchase.

# GRASSI WINE COMPANY

1213 Coombs Street ✦ Napa
Tasting off site, call for details
*Tel:* 707.244.7142 ✦ www.grassiwines.com
Tasting by appointment only

MARK AND JAMI GRASSI, WITH THE HELP OF THEIR DAUGHTER CASSANDRA, MAKE JUST ONE WINE—AROUND 700 cases of a premium cabernet sauvignon ($60) that earned a rating in the 90s from *Wine Spectator* in the first year it was released (2008). Success like that in an area of the world richly blessed with glorious wines—and especially in a region renowned as cabernet country—makes this a wine to watch. If you're looking for something rare and wonderful to take home, something no one else will have heard about, here's your chance.

Part of the secret of the Grassi success is the family vineyards, of course. Devotees of cabernet sauvignon won't be surprised to learn that Silver Oak—something of a legend in Napa County—has a hundred acres of vineyards just behind their property. All the fruit is grown on site here in the Atlas Peak AVA, and, with winemaker Peter Franus (the other part of the Grassi secret), the family makes a wine handcrafted from vineyard to bottle. There is no charge for tasting, and 1% of all proceeds are donated to environmental protection under the One Percent for the Planet program.

# BOUNTY HUNTER WINE BAR AND SMOKIN' BBQ

975 First Street ✦ Napa
Downtown Napa
*Tel* 707.226.3976 ✦ www.bountyhunterwine.com
Daily 11AM to 10PM, later on weekends

**M**ARK POPE IS A SELF-DESCRIBED CROSS BETWEEN CATALOG PIONEER J. PETERMAN, HUMORIST TOM Bodett, and countercultural journalist Hunter S. Thompson, and he is a man with enough irons in the fire to keep all three of those gentlemen intrigued. In addition to his wine catalog sales and impressive range of private label wines, Mark runs one of the quirkiest wine bars, BBQ joints, and wine retail shops in Napa.

Here, you'll find a judicious selection of wines made by the valley's best small vintners, as well as the small-lot wines that Mark buys from contacts in the industry and produces under his own labels, including his flagship Justice (the motto is "Justice Is Served"). If you couldn't fit in as many tasting appointments out on the back lanes as you were hoping, here's a chance to taste some more small-production wines from around the world over a casual lunch or dinner. There are forty wines sold by the glass, another four hundred for sale by the bottle, and hundreds more available by catalog.

If you're hankering for some down-home dining, the menu offers premium meats, cooked out back on the Southern Pride Smoker, including beer-can chicken and Kobe beef burgers, all at reasonable prices (under $20). On weekends, BBQ is served until midnight.

And, as you would expect from a place where luxury meets blue-jeans style, the ambiance alone is worth the trip. The bar rail is an 1887 railroad track from Sheffield, England, and the ceiling is hand-stamped Mexican tin. At the end of one of the tables, an old riding saddle does double duty as a barstool. It's an eccentric, fun watering hole, where you can try out some local wines (or the hand-selected single-barrel bourbons and fine tequilas) and share in the far West vision of a corporate renegade gone cowboy.

# FATTED CALF CHARCUTERIE
# NAPA / OXBOW PUBLIC MARKET

644 First Street ✦ Napa
Downtown Napa
*Tel:* 707.256.3684 ✦ www.fattedcalf.com
Monday *to* Saturday 9AM *to* 7PM, Sunday 10AM *to* 5PM

**T**HE FATTED CALF IS A TEMPLE OF CARNIVOROUS DELIGHTS OFFERING A DIZZYING ARRAY OF CHARCUTERIE MADE according to old-world traditions and using organic and hormone-free meats supplied by local ranchers. If you are planning that gourmet wine country picnic and are wondering where to pick up some wine country *foie gras* before production is banned in 2012—or maybe just a simple *pâté de campagne* or air-cured salami—look no further.

And, while you're at it, it would be a shame to miss the rest of the Oxbow Market. Here in the heart of downtown Napa, there are more than a dozen local purveyors selling everything from specialty teas and fresh-roasted coffees to baked goods, cheese, and local wines. Most vendors stay open late on Tuesday nights, when there is live music along the riverfront.

# ANNALIEN RESTAURANT

1142 Main Street ✦ Napa

Downtown Napa

*Tel:* 707.224.8319

Daily 11:30AM *to* 2PM and 5PM *to* 9PM

THE EXUBERANT OWNER AND CHEF ANNA LIEN COMES FROM THE SOUTHERN REGION OF VIETNAM, AND HER SMALL bistro in downtown Napa serves up some of the valley's best French-Vietnamese cuisine. Her signature dish is sea bass steamed in banana leaf, which has legions of local fans, and other offerings range from steamed dumplings and lemongrass soup to wine-country-inflected dishes such as lamb with lavender sea salt (most dishes $15–25). On hot summer nights, the dining room can get steamy, and there is often a long wait for tables (no reservations accepted). But there's a reason everyone is lined up outside the door, and here in the heart of Napa you can take a leisurely stroll—and maybe even hit one or two of the downtown tasting rooms—while you are waiting for your table.

# PIZZERIA AZZURRO
## E ENOTECA

1260 Main Street ✦ Napa

Downtown Napa

*Tel:* 707.255.5552 ✦ www.azzurropizzeria.com

Monday – Friday 11:30AM – 10PM,

Saturday 5PM – 10PM, Sunday 5PM – 9PM

RUN BY THE HUSBAND-AND-WIFE TEAM OF MICHAEL AND CHRISTINA GYETVAN, PIZZERIA AZZURRO IS A FAVORITE spot in the wine country for wood-fired pizzas served up in a casual and friendly setting. This is the kind of neighborhood restaurant where locals stop by to pick up take-out for the kids and where folks come to celebrate birthdays with friends. There's also a chic wine bar, where you can order up a satisfying meal of antipasti and *bruschette*, a range of fresh salads, and some sinful desserts. Most entrees priced $10–15.

# CHAPTER TWO

# SILVERADO TRAIL

## INCLUDING

## STAG'S LEAP AND OAK KNOLL

### ~WINERIES~

The Silverado Trail runs along the eastern side of the Napa Valley, roughly parallel to the more familiar St. Helena Highway, and connects the city of Napa to the south with Calistoga nearly thirty miles to the north. It was originally established in the nineteenth century as a wagon trail linking the mercury and silver mines on Mount St. Helena with the San Pablo Bay and San Francisco, and today it is one of the wine country's two main tourist itineraries.

More than thirty wineries are clustered along the Silverado Trail, and the road passes through acres of vineyards, making it a popular route for visitors whose tastes run toward the more bucolic. On summer weekends, especially, the traffic and the tasting rooms—although hardly vacant—are often much less congested here than in the more familiar corners of the valley. In the middle parts of the trail, there is only one real convenience store and dining option, the quaint and rustic Soda Canyon Store (4006 Silverado Trail, www.sodacanyonstore.com), and there are almost no gas stations to be found out here, so be sure to fill up the tank before starting out, especially if you plan to go wine tasting over in the mountain valleys, which can be a long way up in the hills. You may want to plan your tasting appointments with a good break for lunch back on the beaten path or pick up the fixings for a gourmet roadside picnic. But once you've got the details arranged, you'll have a whole day to enjoy the sunshine and scenery and some of that famous wine.

# WHITE ROCK VINEYARDS

1115 Loma Vista Drive ✦ Napa
Tasting off site, call for details
Tel: 707.257.7922 ✦ www.whiterockvineyards.com
Tasting by appointment only

ARLY SETTLERS STARTED MAKING WINE ON THE SITE OF
WHITE ROCK VINEYARDS, HERE IN A SMALL VALLEY AT THE
foot of the Stag's Leap range, back in the 1870s. The
Vandendriessche family has been carrying on that tradition in
pastoral seclusion since the 1970s. The winery is located down
at the end of a small lane, well off the beaten path, and you won't find
any sign pointing out the way. Instead, the property is just a broad
expanse of vineyards and oak trees, dotted with the occasional palm tree
and distant barn.

And, when you arrive, there's nothing pretentious. There is a small
laboratory out front, where a bit of the chemistry that it takes to make a
great wine happens, and visitors gather around a small bar tucked back
into the underground *caves* that serve as the production facility and storage rooms at White Rock. Today, building *caves* is something of a fash-
ion in the wine country, but the Vandendriessche family built theirs
twenty years ago. Organic and biodynamic farming is also on the rise in
the Napa Valley, but these vineyards have been managed without herbi-
cides since the 1970s. The result is a winery that feels very much a part
of the scenery that surrounds it, and that's part of the spirit at White
Rock Vineyards.

Owners Claire and Henri released their first commercial vintage

back in the mid-1980s, and they first made their reputation as excellent producers of what they call their Napa Valley claret. In the *Wine Advocate*, Robert Parker recently praised the 2001 vintage for its "distinctive Bordeaux-like personality" and awarded it 90 points. For the first eighteen years, they made just that one red wine and a small-lot production of Burgundian-style chardonnay, with just a whisper of oak. Today, sons Christopher and Michael are now part of the second generation of family winemaking at White Rock, and the Vandendriessches have added two additional cabernet sauvignons, including a reserve wine sold only from the tasting room ($80). There is the occasional release to wine club members of extremely

small lots of other wines—sometimes as few as a half-dozen cases—of viognier, malbec, syrah, and a reserve chardonnay. Most wines are from $30–50, with a total production of around 3,000 cases, and there is no charge for a visit.

The name of the winery comes from the white volcanic ash found in the soil on the property, and, if you've ever been interested in having an insider's look at the volcanic elements of *terroir*, the White Rock caves are a lesson in themselves. The geological striations found along the walls and ceilings of the caves—which range from black lava and red magma to that signature white ash—tell the history of what makes Napa such a uniquely prosperous wine-growing region.

# ROBERT BIALE VINEYARDS

4038 Big Ranch Road ✦ Napa
St. Helena Highway (Highway 29) *to*
Oak Knoll Avenue east, south on Big Ranch Road
*Tel.* 707.257.7555 ✦ www.robertbialevineyards.com
Tasting by appointment only

OBERT PARKER HAS CALLED THIS LITTLE WINERY ONE OF THE MOST ELITE ZINFANDEL PRODUCERS IN CALIFORNIA, and, if you want to taste how wonderful a zinfandel wine can be, this is the place to come. Robert Biale was one of the leaders in the zinfandel revolution of the 1990s, and today the winery's emphasis is still on single-vineyard-designate wines that express the full range of complexity locked up in this versatile grape.

The Biale family has deep roots in the wine country, with the father-and-son team of Aldo and Robert together running the vineyards that Aldo's father, Pietro, started in 1937. Around the turn of the last century, Pietro came to Northern California from Italy, and, after moving to the valley to work a ranch up on Mount Veeder, the family settled on a farm in the town of Napa and planted their vineyards. When Pietro died in a quarry accident in the 1940s, it was left to his teenage son and his widow to run the farm, which the young man did with some verve.

In fact, coming down the lane to the vineyard you'll notice signs with its signature black chicken icon, the name of one of the zinfandels. It's also a nod to Aldo's scofflaw entrepreneurial pluck: Aldo, in his youth, made some delicious homebrew wines from those vineyards—wines that he might have possibly sold without exactly the correct licenses and per-

mits. Back then, telephones used party lines, but, if a caller mentioned how many black chickens were needed, the wine would find its way.

Today, it's Robert Biale and his schoolmate, business partner, and marketer Dave Pramuk, at the helm of the Biale winery. They produce about 10,000 cases per year of wine from the ten-acre estate vineyards in the Oak Knoll District, from the property known simply as "Aldo's Vineyard," and from a variety of historic vineyards, including a block in Sonoma's legendary Monte Rosso vineyard, where some say world-class winemaking in California got its start in the late nineteenth century.

About eighty percent of the production is in the zinfandel that has made the winery famous. *Food & Wine* magazine has, in recent years, twice rated the Black Chicken label as the best zinfandel over $20 in California. There is also a small production of syrah and petite sirah. Wines range from around $40–75, with special pricing (and exclusive event invitations) for the fanatical regulars known as the Black Chicken Society. The charge for a tasting in the working winery, where you can look out over the vineyards and mustard blooms, is $10.

# JUDD'S HILL

2332 Silverado Trail ✦ Napa

Silverado Trail south of the Oak Knoll Avenue intersection

*Tel.* 707.255.2332 ✦ www.juddshill.com

Tasting by appointment only

THERE ARE FEW PLACES IN THE NAPA VALLEY WHERE TASTING IS MORE CONVIVIAL THAN AT JUDD'S HILL. AFTER a meandering drive up through the vineyards, you'll find yourself sitting around a long wooden table, sipping wines, and sharing jokes with new compatriots, who often come from far-flung places around the world. At Judd's Hill, the emphasis is on making wines personally and on creating a personal connection with the people who drink it.

Two generations of the Finkelstein family are at the heart of this family estate: founders Art and Bunnie, their son Judd, and daughter-in-law Holly. Art got his start in winemaking in the early 1970s, making garage wine with his brother in Los Angeles. They took the wines on the county fair circuit, starting bringing home the ribbons, and, before long, went into the wine business together, founding Whitehall Lane. By the late 1980s, the business had grown and was too large to satisfy Art's passion for making small-lot, handcrafted wines, so they sold the winery and started up again at Judd's Hill, with the intention of making just a few thousand cases a year of the wines they enjoyed the most—sauvignon blanc, a summer rosé, pinot noir, petite sirah, and, of course, a Napa Valley cabernet sauvignon (most from $20–45).

The emphasis on the personal, however, goes beyond the tasting room. Judd's Hill hosts a series of lighthearted events throughout the year, and, while wine club members have priority, the remaining tickets are offered to the public. A lobster luau is held in August, a Hanukkah hootenanny in December, and wine cruises up and down the Napa River are scheduled around the harvest. The winery's hospitality director, Pat Burke, is a national BBQ champion, whose dry rub earned him the 2007 West Coast Rib Championship. Those interested in joining the fun can check the web site for details. While you're on the web site, don't miss taking a peek at the weekly installment of Judd's Enormous Wine Show—an insider's comic view on the world of wine.

If you want to take home wine with your own stamp on it, Judd's Hill also offers another hands-on opportunity to learn a bit more about the art of winemaking and to make your own custom-crafted wines. In most cases, the process starts with a blending seminar, with the winemaker guiding you through the process of mixing different varietals to balance the flavors and components of a finished wine, and ends with you bottling and corking your vintage (prices from $195).

The tasting fee at Judd's Hill is $10, waived with a purchase of $45 of more. Unlike many places in the valley, the winery is kid-friendly.

# CASA NUESTRA WINERY

3451 Silverado Trail ✦ St. Helena
Silverado Trail north of the Deer Park Road intersection
*Tel:* 707.963.5783 ✦ www.casanuestra.com
Tasting by appointment only

ASA NUESTRA MEANS SIMPLY "OUR HOUSE," AND A FOLKSY COUNTRY WELCOME IS THE HALLMARK AT THIS SMALL AND progressively run winery owned by Gene Kirkham and Cody Gillette Kirkham—the good friends and former marital partners who first established Casa Nuestra back in 1979. Located down a gravel lane on the west side of the Silverado Trail, the tasting room here is a quirky old farmhouse, where bellying up to the bar means gathering in front of weathered boards set out across a vintage desk.

The philosophy here is that wine is liquid art and that community values are what sustain us. This means that the eight stars on each label recognize the winery's eight dedicated employees, the wooden packing boxes are made by disabled adults, and the clothing with the winery logo is made from hemp and bamboo. The grapes in the vineyards out back are grown organically, and, in these days when water is becoming a scarce commodity in Cali-

fornia, Casa Nuestra is moving toward dry farming—raising grapes without any supplemental irrigation.

Apart from local restaurant sales, distribution is almost exclusively from the tasting room, and if you're looking for a chance to try some rare varietals and unusual blends, Casa Nuestra has a lot to offer. Thirty years ago, the winery developed one of the first cabernet franc programs in North America, and many of the other vines it grows—alicante bouché, carignan, French colombard—remain specialty grapes in Napa. The estate chenin blanc has been praised by *Wine Spectator*'s Matt Kramer as the "finest and truest California chenin blanc"; other favorites include a dry rosé, a tinto classico red blend, an old vine petite sirah, a dry riesling, and a special late-harvest French colombard (wines from $16–55). For enthusiasts looking to sample these off-beat wines on a regular basis, good discounts are offered through the wine club, Club Casa.

The winemaker's tasting includes a walk down the lane to the estate winery, a tour of the vineyards, and a special vineyard surprise. Elvis Presley fans may remember that the opening scene of his 1962 film *Wild in the Country* was filmed in the wine country, and, that's right, this was the location. The tasting room includes an offbeat collection of Presley memorabilia, most donated by enthusiastic visitors to this small family winery. The total production is around 2,000 cases a year. The tasting fee is $10, refundable with a purchase.

# HUNNICUTT WINES

3524 Silverado Trail North ✦ St. Helena
Silverado Trail south of the Bale Lane intersection
*Tel:* 707.963.2911 ✦ www.hunnicuttwines.com
Tasting Tuesday *to* Sunday 10AM *to* 5PM, by appointment only

USTIN HUNNICUTT STEPHENS RELEASED HIS FIRST WINES,
A CABERNET SAUVIGNON AND A ZINFANDEL, IN 2004, BUT
he was no stranger to the winemaking industry. His father
had started producing wines in the 1990s from a Howell
Mountain St. Helena estate property under the family's D. R.
Stephens Estate label, which Justin also manages and co-owns, and his
first job in the wine business was learning the ropes in the cellars at one
of the other local wineries.

That first year, Justin produced
fewer than 250 cases of wine under
the Hunnicutt label; these days the
focus is still on making small lots of
premium wines. The annual production currently is around 2,000 cases,
focusing mainly on cabernet sauvignon, along with a chardonnay, a
zinfandel, a syrah, a merlot, and a proprietary blend of petite sirah called
Fearless Red (wines from $25–95).

The new Hunnicutt tasting room is
located on the Silverado Trail just a

few minutes from downtown St. Helena, where you can talk wines with Justin and his wife Seana (and eventually their daughter Parker), and enjoy discovering some new favorites in a relaxed environment. You can belly up to the tasting bar for a convivial experience, or there are café tables overlooking the gardens and pine trees if you're looking to set a more leisurely pace. The visit includes a behind-the-scenes production tour, the chance to try some barrel samples, and a tasting of some of the finished wines. The $25 fee is waived with purchases of $100.

# FAILLA WINES

3530 Silverado Trail North ✦ St. Helena
Silverado Trail south of the Bale Lane intersection
*Tel.* 707.963.0530 ✦ www.faillawines.com
Tasting by appointment only

**R**UN BY THE HUSBAND-AND-WIFE TEAM OF EHREN JORDAN AND ANNE-MARIE FAILLA, FAILLA WINES (PRONOUNCED fay-la) consistently produces world-class wines, but there's no mistaking that this is a family business. The *San Francisco Chronicle* named Ehren—who, in addition to crafting the wines at Failla, is also the winemaker at Turley Wine Cellars—the 2008 winemaker of the year. The Faila 2006 Napa Valley Phoenix Ranch syrah was first on *Wine Spectator*'s Top 100 Wines list in 2008. But on weekends you are likely to see their children riding bicycles out back.

Failla's first estate vineyards were on the Sonoma Coast; in 2004 they purchased the ten-acre property just off the Silverado Trail. By 2008, Ehren and Anne-Marie had completed construction of an underground production facility and converted the old farmhouse to an inviting and cheerful tasting room. A visit to Failla still feels like being invited into a winemaker's home, and tasting often takes place sitting around a coffee table in comfortable armchairs and couches. The shady veranda has views of the vineyards.

Ehren makes around 5,000 cases of wine a year, mostly Sonoma Coast and Napa Valley pinot noir. There is also a smaller production of chardonnay, syrah, and viognier. Wines range from around $35–65, and the $10 tasting fee is waived with purchase.

# HAGAFEN CELLARS

4160 Silverado Trail ✦ Napa

Silverado Trail just south of the Oak Knoll Avenue intersection

*Tel.* 888.424.2336 ✦ www.hagafen.com

Tasting by appointment only

FOUNDED BY THE HUSBAND-AND-WIFE TEAM OF ERNIE AND IRIT WEIR IN 1979, THE WINE COUNTRY HAS GROWN UP around Hagafen Cellars. Today, this small family winery is surrounded by some of the valley's great commercial giants, but they have determinedly retained their hands-on approach to the small-lot production of sustainably produced Napa Valley wines.

The family grows walnuts and fruits in the orchard out behind the tasting room (available free-for-the-taking to tasting room visitors in season), and they keep an organic kitchen garden on the property. The name Hagafen comes from the Hebrew *borei pri hagafen*, which translates to "blessed are the fruits of the vine" and is the idea at the heart of the Weirs' approach to the wine-making business.

The 2008 vintage marked the thirtieth anniversary of commercial wine production at Hagafen, where the family makes twenty-eight different

wines for a total of 8,000 cases annually. That means, of course, that these are small-lot wines, each handcrafted and a labor of love. On offer are an award-winning estate Riesling and a crisp sauvignon blanc, a range of pinot noir and cabernet sauvignon wines, including several single-vineyard-designate and reserve wines suitable for cellaring (prices from around $15–75).

This is the kind of tasting room where everyone is welcome—from serious collectors to first-time wine tasters. There is room out on the back patio to accommodate larger groups if you are looking for a perfect setting for a more expansive wine-country event. The feeling here is low-key, casual, and friendly. The tasting fee is $5 for the signature tasting and $10 for the reserve tasting, and the fee is refunded with purchase.

# PHIFER PAVITT WINE

4660 Silverado Trail ✦ Calistoga
Silverado Trail, just north of the Dunaweal Lane intersection
*Tel:* 707.942.4787 ✦ www.phiferpavittwine.com
Tasting by appointment only

**S**UZANNE AND SHANE PHIFER PAVITT MAKE JUST 300 CASES AND ONE WINE (AROUND $80), BUT THAT RELEASE—called simply Date Night—is already one of Napa's most celebrated cabernet sauvignons. When you consider that Napa is justly famous for its world-class cabernet sauvignon wines, that's saying something. The debut release in 2008, made by winemaker

Ted Osborne (with help from Shane's father, Gary Warburton), from organic fruit sourced in Pope Valley, earned stellar accolades. The *San Francisco Chronicle* ranked it in the year's top 100 wines, and *Wine Spectator* gave the inaugural effort an impressive 90 points. The wine is blended with just a whisper of petit verdot.

While this is a serious wine lover's wine, the attitude at Phifer Pavitt is completely down-to-earth and lighthearted, a spirit reflected in everything from the cowgirl

on the wine label to the relaxed atmosphere in the new tasting room. The wine gets its name from the couple's weekly date night, where they swear all the best decisions are made.

# VENGE VINEYARDS

4708 Silverado Trail ✦ Calistoga
Silverado Trail, south of the Pickett Road intersection
*Tel.* 707.942.9100 ✦ www.vengevineyards.com
Tasting by appointment only

**K**IRK VENGE GREW UP IN A WINEMAKING FAMILY AND GOT HIS FIRST INTRODUCTION TO MANAGING VINEYARDS riding around on tractors as a boy. From there, a life in the wine industry was a natural choice, and, after working a harvest Down Under and completing two degrees at the University of California at Davis, he returned to the valley where he grew up.

Today, Kirk is the proprietor and winemaker at Venge Vineyards, just off the Silverado Trail, where he farms the twelve-and-a-half-acre property that he purchased in 2008. On the approach to the estate, visitors meander past neatly trimmed vineyards on the way up to the ranch-house-turned-tasting-salon, where dogs Lucy and Remy offer a friendly greeting and you'll get a chance to taste some wines. Kirk is passionate about making wines, and, if he's not out in the vineyards, it's easy to get him talking about what a bit of charbono, syrah, and sangiovese add to his zinfandel blend or how native yeasts help to create wine with a unique sense of place.

At Venge, the total production is fewer than 4,000 cases a year. Kirk makes ten different wines, including a signature reserve Napa Valley cabernet sauvignon, a chardonnay, and a late-harvest zinfandel, in the $26–125 range. From the sweeping shaded veranda of the tasting room there are views across the valley to Diamond Mountain, and on a sunny afternoon it's a great spot to unwind for a bit before returning to the tasting trail.

# JAMES COLE WINERY

5014 Silverado Trail ✦ Napa
Silverado Trail at Oak Knoll Crossroad
*Tel.* 707.251.9905 ✦ www.jamescolewinery.com
Tasting daily 10AM *to* 5PM, by appointment only

I N THE BARREL ROOM AT THE JAMES COLE WINERY, WHAT YOU SEE LINED UP ALONG THE WALLS IS THE ENTIRE VINTAGE, AND these are not wines you are going to find anywhere else. Because James Cole—the dream of James and Colleen Harder—still makes fewer than 1,000 cases a year, all of it sold directly from the winery. This is a strictly word-of-mouth sort of place, where you won't find

balloons out front or gimmicks in the tasting room. But the people who discover the Harders come back, vintage after vintage, and that's exactly the idea. The sign above the bar in the tasting room reads simply "enter as strangers, leave as friends."

James and Colleen met on a blind date after college, when James was on a business trip to Napa and Colleen was living in San Francisco. James had experience running a winery in his native Canada, and a mutual friend suggested, fatefully it would seem, that they meet for a glass of wine. When they later bought their estate vineyards and tasting room site here on the Silverado Trail, the property was a run-down horse ranch, which the couple has since transformed into a winery and chic tasting room. They currently make wines in the $30–125 range, including a 100% estate cabernet sauvignon, some small lots of 100% malbec and 100% petit verdot, and a serious—and seriously drinkable—chardonnay. The tasting experience ($20) is hands-on and personalized, and, although the Silverado Trail is not precisely a remote back lane, James Cole is a far cry from the great din of the busy commercial wineries along this famous wine route.

# SHAFER VINEYARDS

6154 Silverado Trail ✦ Napa
Silverado Trail just south of the Yountville Cross Road
*Tel:* 707.944.2877 ✦ www.shafervineyards.com
Tasting by appointment only

WHEN FOLKS START TALKING ABOUT THE WINEMAKERS WHO CHANGED THE HISTORY OF NAPA IN THE 1970s and who put the wines from this narrow valley on the world map, the first names to come to mind might be Robert Mondavi, Louis Martini, and Bob Trinchero (who famously invented white zinfandel). But, for many people in the valley, one of the names that comes to mind next is John Shafer. After serving with the Air Force and flying missions to Germany during the last months of the World War II, followed by a career in publishing, he bought a 210-acre ranch in the wine country and moved his family west in 1972.

He was forty-eight years old, and for the first six years the family grew grapes, while John threw himself into learning the craft of winemaking. His first commercial release of cabernet sauvignon won the prestigious San Francisco Vintners Club tasting competition. Within a decade, Shafer wines were outranking some of the legendary *premier cru* Bordeaux wines, at a moment when suddenly the wine world's attention was turning to Napa.

Currently Shafer produces around 30,000 cases of wine a year, and, with a stunning hillside tasting room right off the famed Silverado Trail, it would be hard to claim Shafer as an undiscovered secret. Today, run by John and his middle son Doug, this is very much still an intimate

family business. In the tasting room, wines are served in "flights," with an array of gleaming glassware and gorgeous views over the vineyards. No jostling at a crowded tasting bar: this is a chance to participate in an expert wine seminar and to see what a small family business can accomplish after forty years of hard work.

The family is still renowned for its Hillside Select cabernet, an opulent wine made of 100% cabernet that retails for over $200. But you'll also taste from their range of chardonnay, merlot, cabernet, and syrah wines, and they often pour samples of their recent production of 100% hillside cabernet port (most wines $50–70). Business travelers and home gourmets will appreciate the half-bottles, which make it possible to enjoy a fine wine for one or a different vintage with every course. These are classic California wines, with big, ripe flavors.

The winery is completely solar-powered, and the vineyard tour that begins the tasting takes place overlooking Stag's Leap. The fee for tasting is $45, and generally appointments need to be made several weeks in advance.

# ROBERT SINSKEY VINEYARDS

6320 Silverado Trail ✦ Napa

Silverado Trail just south of the Yountville Cross Road

*Tel:* 707.944.9090 ✦ www.robertsinskey.com

Tasting daily 10AM to 4:30PM, tours by appointment

FROM THE TASTING BAR AT ROBERT SINSKEY, THE VIEW LOOKS DIRECTLY ONTO THE WORKING WINERY; THIS INTEGRATED approach to the experience of wine is the hallmark of this family vineyard, which released its first vintage in 1986. Although the annual production is approaching 25,000 cases,

this is still a small, hands-on winery, the kind of place where, come January, everyone in the cellar takes a turn out back with the bottling.

Founded by Robert Sinskey *père* and now run by the husband-and-wife team of Robert Jr. and chef and cookbook author Maria Helm Sinskey, the winery produces certified organic and biodynamically farmed estate wines, and the emphasis is—perhaps unsurprisingly—on making clean, easy-to-drink vintages that pair well with food. The tasting experience is accompanied by house-made *hors d'oeuvres* made using Maria's recipes, with many of the ingredients grown in the large gardens out in front of the winery. In the autumn, the kitchens out back are busy with canning and making some of the homemade fruit jams for sale in the winery. In addition to wine tasting, seasonal culinary tours and occasional wine-country cooking events are held.

Nineteen different wines are on offer, all small-lot productions—
sometimes as little as forty or fifty cases. Robert Sinskey is known for
pinot noir wines made from properties in the Carneros, but the
winery also makes several different Bordeaux blends, a range of
white wines, and an especially delicious late-harvest Alsatian-style

dessert wine made from pinot gris. As the staff will tell you, they are proud of the fact that there is no advertising budget at Robert Sinskey; the reputation for excellent wines has been built by word of mouth and by the friendly welcome visitors will discover. Tasting fees around $20.

# PIÑA NAPA VALLEY

8060 Silverado Trail
Silverado Trail north of the Oakville Cross Road
*Tel:* 707.738.9328 ✦ www.pinanapavalley.com
Tasting by appointment only

THE PIÑA FAMILY HAS BEEN FARMING VINEYARDS IN THE NAPA VALLEY FOR SIX GENERATIONS, AND TODAY FOUR Piña siblings—John, Larry, Ranndy, and Davie—run this family winery. While the family made its fortunes for many years in vineyard management and ranching, in the 1960s father John established a family estate here on the Silverado Trail, and the brothers now source their grapes from select vineyards throughout the county.

The emphasis is on single-vineyard-designate cabernet sauvignon blends (most around $80), and recent releases have earned solid points in the 90s in places such as *Wine Enthusiast*. Wine tasting at the Piña winery includes a tour of the barrel rooms, where you can soak in the pungent, clean scent of oak, and learn how a wine evolves in the aging and blending process. On summer days, there are patio tables and umbrellas where you can relax and look out over the Silverado Trail, and if you're in luck, the fire pit will be burning, cooking up something special at one of the winery's club events or open houses. There is no charge for tasting.

# GHOST WINERIES

NAPA'S MODERN REPUTATION AS A PREMIUM WINE REGION DATES FROM THE 1970s, WHEN A SMALL GROUP of pioneering vintners made their way onto the world stage with wines that started winning some of the industry's most prestigious tasting contests. But this was not a new development in the county—it was a return to a winemaking tradition that had flourished in Napa more than a hundred years earlier. By the 1860s, the Napa Valley was renowned as a grape-growing region, and the wines made here were exported around the world. By the turn of the twentieth century, it was already a tourist destination. Then came Prohibition, which stymied the winemaking culture and the local economic engine for a generation. Vineyards were pulled up and replanted with fruit orchards. Wineries went out of business, and the buildings were turned to hay barns, left abandoned, or sometimes stealthily burnt to the ground for insurance money. And winemaking in much of Napa was on hold until the renaissance of the 1970s.

But not all the vineyards were destroyed. A small proportion of those early plantings survived on family ranches, and today a handful of producers offer "old vine" wines made from pre-Prohibition vineyards. Not all the wineries fell to ruin either. Those that survived are known simply as "ghost wineries." Sometimes they are abandoned properties in the midst of vineyards, where you can take a twilight tour and experience shades of old Napa. Sometimes they have been converted to new uses. But, increasingly, the ghost wineries are being restored to active production, largely due to local efforts in historic preservation and due to a licensing regulation that makes the expensive and complicated process of bonding a new winery in the valley vastly simpler for any owner who can prove that an historic winemaking facility once existed on the property. Today, there are several dozen active ghost wineries in the Napa Valley, each with a storied past, and there are likely to be more in the decades to come.

# CHAPTER THREE

# CALISTOGA
## AND ENVIRONS

**L**ocated at the far northern end of the Napa Valley, Calistoga today is famous for its bottled water and for its historic mineral hot springs, where you can soak away your cares and, some say, revitalize your health in waters heated by underground geysers. As the legend goes, the city got its name when the entrepreneurial pioneer Sam Brannan set about establishing a resort that he proposed to market to the world as the Saratoga Springs of California. By a slip of the tongue, Calistoga was born.

Today, Calistoga is also a laid-back and slightly offbeat place, with a charming main street, plenty of small restaurants, and some quirky boutique shopping. There are remarkably few tasting rooms set up in the town center, but there are plenty of small wineries tucked away in the outskirts of town, along the northern reaches of the St. Helena Highway and the Silverado Trail, and if you're looking for a relaxed pace—made even more relaxing by a luxury spa treatment—it's a perfect place to while away an afternoon.

# MADRIGAL VINEYARDS

3718 St. Helena Highway ✦ Calistoga
St. Helena Highway (Highway 29) between
Larkmead Lane and Bale Lane intersections
*Tel.* 707.942.6577 ✦ www.madrigalvineyards.com
Tasting by appointment only

THE MADRIGALS HAVE BEEN DEVELOPING VINEYARD EXPER-
TISE HERE IN NAPA SINCE 1939, WHEN THE FIRST MEMBERS
of the family emigrated from Mexico to work the harvests.
After decades of working in vineyard management and selling
the fruit from their forty-acre estate property, the family has
now moved into winemaking as well. Madrigal released its first
commercial vintage in 1995, a mere 500 cases, and a little more than a
decade later its petite sirah wine ($35) has a cult following in the valley.

Today, the winery, under the direction of owners Jess and Chris Madrigal, produces around 5,000 cases of wine, which includes, in addition to
their petite sirah, a range of zinfandel, merlot, chardonnay, and cabernet
wines, as well as a petite sirah port-style dessert wine and a Bordeaux
blend known as Sonnet #63 (most wines from $26–60). *Wine Spectator*
gave the reserve cabernet—Las Viñas del Señor—a stellar 91 points in
2009, which has only added to this little winery's growing reputation.

The family has recently opened a new tasting room just off the St.
Helena Highway, where visitors are treated to a tour and tasting in the
traditional California-style stucco winery. The estate vineyards begin
out back, and the production takes place on site. The fee for tasting is
$20, refunded with purchase.

# SHYPOKE

2882A Foothill Boulevard ✦ Calistoga
St. Helena Highway (Highway 29) at the Heitz Way intersection
*Tel.* 707.942.0420 ✦ www.shypoke.com
Tasting by appointment only

CHARBONO IS AN ITALIAN GRAPE THAT GENETIC TESTING TRACES BACK TO THE SAVOY REGION OF FRANCE, WHERE IT was known as charbonneau. In California, it is often known simply as "Calistoga's Grape," because this northern corner of the Napa Valley is one of the world's best regions for growing this increasingly rare vine.

At Shypoke, the Heitz Family, who has owned vineyard property in the Napa Valley since 1896, has been growing charbono for more than a hundred years and is one of the wine country's largest producers of the varietal. They make around 700 cases a year. If you've never tried a charbono—and chances are you haven't—a visit to this small, family-run winery is a chance to taste something unique and wonderful.

A great-grandfather purchased this fifty-acre ranch at the end of

the nineteenth century, and the family made wine from the charbono vineyards until Prohibition put them out of business. While most of the property was converted to orchards, a couple of acres of the original vineyards survived, and in the 1950s they started replanting the land to grapes again, primarily charbono with smaller lots of cabernet sauvignon, sangiovese, and petite sirah.

Today, the winery is run by two generations of the Heitz family, who, because they don't have to pay a monstrous mortgage on a piece of vineyard property, can afford to produce excellent wines at very reasonable prices. The wines are all under $35.

The grapes are farmed using sustainable practices—the family says it doesn't want vineyards where they have to worry about their kids playing out back in the fields. The crush takes place in winemaker Peter Heitz's small barn in Calistoga using a hand-cranked basket press. The family also donates one percent of its sales to environmental causes. There are vegetable gardens behind the house and free-range chickens in the vineyards, and, if you come when things are busy, you just might be put to work. If you're lucky, the wood-fired pizza oven will be going.

The Shypoke name comes from a local folk term for the blue herons that make their home along the river. The cool nights here in Calistoga produce fruits that ripen slowly. These are wines made with a light touch. The current production is right around a thousand cases, and there's no charge for a tasting appointment.

# ZAHTILA VINEYARDS

2250 Lake County Highway ✦ Calistoga

Silverado Trail & Lake County Highway (Highway 29),
north of Calistoga

*Tel.* 707.942.9451 ✦ www.zahtilavineyards.com

Tasting by appointment only

F OR CENTURIES, WINEMAKING HAS LARGELY BEEN A MAN'S WORLD, AND THAT HAS BEEN AS TRUE HISTORICALLY IN the new wine country of Northern California as much as in the old world of France and Italy. But Laura Zahtila, the one-woman-show behind Zahtila Vineyards, is one of those rare exceptions—she's never been one to follow the beaten path.

After spending seventeen years working in the high-tech industry, she and her then-husband stumbled across a winery for sale, and it changed her life.

After their third harvest, she found herself divorced, and, instead of seeing it as the end of a dream, she was determined to make a life in the wine world as a single woman. Not having grown up in the vineyards, she brought in consultant winemakers to help define the Zahtila house style. Now, a little more than a de-

cade after she first set foot on the property, she is making 3,000 cases of premium Napa Valley wine—a chardonnay, two zinfandels, two cabernets, and a dessert wine that changes with each vintage. Wines start at under $20 and go up to $95 for the reserve cabernet.

Tasting takes place at a redwood bar in a converted—although you would never know it—garage. Designed to resemble the traditional bar-style wineries that are so familiar on the back lanes of the wine country, the tasting room is entered through a door framed by an old wisteria vine. Out front, there is a profusion of hydrangeas and a sprawling rose garden, where Laura grows more than three hundred different rose plants, which bloom in fragrant splendor from April through September. There are plenty of winery cats luxuriating in the sunshine and, if you're looking for a lighthearted souvenir, whimsical "Wine Chick" t-shirts are for sale in the tasting room. The tasting fee is $10 and includes a souvenir wine glass.

# AUGUST BRIGGS WINERY

333 Silverado Trail ✦ Calistoga
Silverado Trail just south of the town of Calistoga
*Tel:* 707.942.4912 ✦ www.augustbriggswines.com
Tasting daily 10:30AM to 4:30PM

**A**S YOU HEAD SOUTH FROM CALISTOGA—UNDOUBTEDLY RELAXED AFTER A LEISURELY LUNCH OR A LONG SOAK IN one of the town's famous mineral hot springs—you'll see the red-tin-roofed winery of August Briggs set just back from the head of the Silverado Trail. It would be a shame to miss trying some of their wines because it's one of the relatively few back lane places in the valley where you can visit without an appointment (and there's no charge for wine tasting, either). You're likely to meet the owner and proprietor, August "Joe" Briggs, who produced his first commercial vintage back in 1995, after having worked for more than a decade in winemaking up and down the West Coast, where he developed a reputation for his skill with pinot noir.

Today, Joe runs the business with the help of his two nephews, Jessie and Aaron. This small family team handles everything from the crush to the tasting room, though other members of the family, including his parents and his wife Sally, pitch in during the harvest, which is always one of the busiest and most exuberant times of the year here in the wine country.

The winery celebrated its first estate harvest on the property just outside the Calistoga city limits in 2004; it currently produces something under 7,000 cases of wine a year, sourced from twenty different vine-

yards. The petite sirah is grown in the two-acre estate vineyard just beyond the tasting room doors, and there are four different pinot noir wines, several cabernet sauvignons, syrah, and, more unusually, both a pinot meunier and a charbono.

Wine aficionados will recognize pinot meunier as one of the three grapes allowed in French champagne production (the others being the more familiar pinot noir and chardonnay varietals), and, although it is one of the most broadly planted grapes in France, you won't often find it bottled separately. Charbono, meanwhile, is known as "Calistoga's Grape," and in the nineteenth and early twentieth centuries it was a common varietal. Today, vineyards planted to the grape are dwindling, but the area's unique microclimate has long been recognized as an ideal area for growing this dark red grape, which boasts a distinctive plum aroma. It makes a delicious wine.

August Briggs is a working winery and tasting room in one—the tasting room opens onto the production area where the barrels are aged on site. If you're looking for a warm welcome and an introduction to some of the finer points of winemaking, it's a great place to drop in and ask some questions. The folks pouring your wines are disarmingly good natured and expert all at once—and likely as not they are part of the Briggs family, responsible for making the wine you get to enjoy.

# LAVA VINE

965 Silverado Trail ✦ Calistoga
Silverado Trail just south of the
Lake County Highway (Highway 29) intersection
*Tel:* 707.942.9500 ✦ www.lavavine.com
Tasting daily 10AM to 5PM

WHEN JILL AND JOE CABRAL MOVED TO THE NAPA VALLEY IN THE MID-1990s, MAKING WINE WASN'T PART of their plan. She worked as an interior designer, and he ran a construction company. But when Jill's mother bought a piece of property up in Calistoga with an old port vineyard on it, Joe started making his first wines, and before long his hobby became a passion. In 2006, the couple released their first vintage, working with winemaker Nile Zacherle (whose own wines, under the Zacherle label, are also poured at the Lava Vine tasting room). Just a few years later, they opened their tasting room at the head of the Silverado Trail.

The Cabral family today produces around a thousand cases a year of premium, handcrafted wines, sourcing their mostly organic fruit from vineyards in the Knights Valley and Spring Mountain appellations. These wines have those intense mountain tannins and the earthy dark fruits that have made the hillside wines of Napa famous. Currently, they make syrah, cabernet sauvignon, viognier, and port wines (around $35–50), and there are plans eventually to include a petite sirah in the line-up.

The $10 charge for tasting is waived with purchase, and a dollar from

every case sold in the tasting room is donated to the Lung Cancer Alliance. For anyone who couldn't quite get away from it all on the tasting trip, the winery welcomes well-behaved children and dogs.

# ZACHERLE WINES

965 Silverado Trail ✦ Calistoga
Silverado Trail just south of the
Lake County Highway (Highway 29) intersection
*Tel:* 707.942.9500 ✦ www.zacherlewines.com
Tasting daily 10AM to 5PM

NILE ZACHERLE'S FIRST LOVE WASN'T WINE BUT BEER. SOMETIME WELL BEFORE HE REACHED TWENTY-ONE, HE started making beer at home with his father, and, when he went off to college at the University of California at Davis, it was to study in the master brewers program. Along the way, he added a degree in fermentation science to his credentials as a master brewer. In the years since, Nile has worked as a winemaker at some of Napa's premium estates, including Barnett Vineyards, S. E. Chase, and the celebrated Château Montelena—whose 1973 vintage famously beat out its storied French competitors in the "Judgment of Paris." After taking some time to make wines in Bordeaux, France and Margaret River, Australia, he teamed up with his wife, Whitney Fisher, also the winemaker and vineyards manager at her family's winery, Fisher Vineyards.

Today, Nile continues to work as a consulting winemaker for a number of projects in the valley, making around 500 cases a year of small-production wines under the Zacherle label, which wine aficionados can sample at the Lava Vine tasting room. Current releases include viognier, syrah, and port-style dessert wines from Knights Valley, a cabernet sauvignon from Mount Veeder, and a syrah from the Spring Mountain district (prices from around $30–90). There is no charge for individual visits to the tasting room.

# T VINE CELLARS

P.O. Box 1115 ✦ Calistoga
Tasting off site, call for details
*Tel:* 707.942.8685 ✦ www.tvinecellars.com
Tasting by appointment only

REG BROWN DISCOVERED GRENACHE ON A WINE TASTING TRIP IN FRANCE. ONE AFTERNOON HE WENT INTO A SMALL wine shop to ask for a recommendation, and the man behind the counter started talking about one of the local wines with the enthusiasm most guys reserve for a beautiful woman. What was there to do but buy the wine and immediately drink it? And, after that, what else but to come home, quit a job in high finance, and start studying wine and winemaking in earnest?

Greg started out working in cellars, dragging hoses for $6 an hour, and learned the craft of winemaking from the ground up. In the early 1990s, he released his first production—two hundred cases of grenache. Now, T Vine Cellars—the T stands for the trinity of body, mind, and spirit that goes into the appreciation of any great vintage—makes around 4,500 cases annually and nine different highly acclaimed wines. In 2002, the *San Francisco Chronicle* proclaimed this the best syrah in the world, and there's a plaque to prove it somewhere down in the cellar. The wines sell out every year, and, to get a bottle of some of the most coveted releases, you'll have to join the allocation list, because the ethos here is staying loyal to the people who have been loyal to them.

These days the hillside tasting rooms do double duty as a working winery and barrel storage facility. This is one of the few places where visitors are welcome during the crush, but be warned, if they are busy, someone will put a pitchfork in your hand—this is the kind of place where everyone helps out during the harvest. The grapes are sourced from the small farms of independent growers around the county, and business deals are based on handshakes and hugs rather than a lot of paperwork.

The wines ($30–55) are mostly Bordeaux and Rhône varietals—a syrah, petite sirah, two different zinfandels, some cabernet and merlot wines, and, of course, grenache. There is no charge for tasting.

# VOCES

P.O. Box 687 ✦ Calistoga
Tasting off site, call for details
*Tel:* 707.225.2474 ✦ www.voceswine.com
Tasting at T Vine Cellars, by appointment only

**F**ERNANDO CANDELARIO DESCRIBES HIMSELF AS "MEXICAN, WINEMAKER, DREAMER," AND HIS STORY IS ONE THAT YOU hear more and more often in the Napa Valley. His parents came to the wine country from Mexico to work in the vineyards, and he grew up in the industry. He started out in the 1990s bottling wines in the cellars and today is the assistant winemaker and cellar master at T Vine Cellars, where proprietor Greg Brown encourages anyone with a dream about wine to give it a try.

So, since 2001, Fernando has been making a small amount of hand-crafted wine under the Voces label. He currently produces around 700 cases a year of three varietals—a petite sirah, a cabernet sauvignon, and a zinfandel ($40). These wines have found a place on the wine lists of prestigious restaurants including New York City's Per Se and Napa Valley's Martini House, but otherwise the only distribution is through the tasting room or the web site. There is no charge for tasting.

# SOLBAR

755 Silverado Trail ✦ Calistoga
At the Solage Calistoga Resort
*Tel:* 866.942.7442 ✦ www.solagecalistoga.com
Daily 7AM *to* 11PM, closed 3PM *to* 5PM

THE RESORT AT SOLAGE CALISTOGA IS DELIGHTFULLY POSH, AND, IF YOU ARE LOOKING FOR A HIGH-END, LUXURY retreat in the wine country, this is the place to go. But if your budget doesn't quite stretch to a couple of hundred bucks for a spa treatment, do what the locals do and visit Solbar, the resort's open-to-the-public restaurant, for lunch or a late afternoon cocktail. Most entrees are around $15, there's a good local wine list, the setting is simply lovely, and, best of all, there are bocce courts where you can stake the check on a little friendly competition.

# HYDRO BAR & GRILL

1403 Lincoln Avenue ✦ Calistoga

Downtown Calistoga

*Tel:* 707.942.9777

Daily 8:30AM *to* 10PM

IF YOU'RE IN THE MOOD FOR CASUAL BAR-STYLE FOOD IN A RELAXED ATMOSPHERE, HYDRO IS AN EXCELLENT WATERING hole. With a broad selection of local and international beers on tap, it can also be just the thing when you find yourself thinking you couldn't possibly quaff another glass of the valley's famed wines. Located right on the main street in Calistoga, you can stop by for a gourmet burger, munch on some white-truffle-oil fries, and plan the next stage of your tasting itinerary.

Even better, if you are wondering what to do after-hours when the tasting rooms are closed, stop by for the live music on weekends (Fridays and Saturdays from 9PM, Sundays from 7PM). Local blues bands play tunes, and area residents turn out for the entertainment.

# CALMART

1491 Lincoln Avenue ✦ Calistoga

Downtown Calistoga

*Tel.* 707.942.9686 ✦ www.calmartnv.com

**H**ERE IN THE WINE COUNTRY, EVEN THE LOCAL GROCERY STORE CAN BE A DELIGHTFUL GOURMET EXPERIENCE, AND the owners of the CalMart in downtown Calistoga have done their best to make sure no one walks away hungry. This unpretentious little grocery—where the community does its daily marketing—is stocked with local provisions, a fine wine selection, and all the fixings anyone would ever need to put together an unsurpassed shopping bag luncheon or romantic picnic. The store also offers catering by request.

# CALISTOGA SPA HOT SPRINGS

1006 Washington Street ✦ Calistoga
Downtown Calistoga
707.942.6269 ✦ www.calistogaspa.com
Daily 10AM *to* 9PM

CALISTOGA IS NAPA VALLEY'S ULTIMATE HOT SPOT. FOR MORE THAN A CENTURY, THIS SMALL TOWN ON THE northern end of the tasting trail has been famous for its natural hot springs, and the area is dotted with resorts and spas offering mud baths, beauty treatments, and long soaks in the mineral pools. While there are spas more upscale and elegant than the Calistoga Spa Hot Springs, this is the place the locals come, especially in the evenings after 7PM when the price is reduced to just $10 (day passes $25). Four large pools are naturally heated to different temperatures, and folks bring picnics and bottles of wine to share at the tables. On long summer nights, you can lounge poolside with a book or just take in the atmosphere. Massage and spa treatments are available by appointment.

# INDIAN SPRINGS RESORT

1712 Lincoln Avenue ✦ Calistoga

Downtown Calistoga

*Tel:* 707.942.4913 ✦ www.indianspringscalistoga.com

Daily 9AM *to* 8PM

I CAN NEVER DECIDE WHICH I LIKE BETTER, THE HOT SPRINGS AT THE CALISTOGA SPA OR THE LUXURIOUS POOLS AT INDIAN Springs, so the best recommendation is to try both. Of the two, Indian Springs is a bit more fancy—although by Napa standards this is still very much a down-to-earth kind of place. Driving into the resort you'll begin to wonder if you've stepped back in time, when California was still old Hollywood and everything was just a bit more glamorous.

There is just one mineral pool, dating to 1917, but it is large and spacious. You can easily spend a day paddling about, tanning poolside, and drinking the signature cucumber water. Day passes to the pool are around $20, a full range of spa treatments are offered, including mud baths and massage, and excellent winter packages extend tempting discounts. If you book a room at one of the charming resort cottages, you have late-night and complimentary access to the hot springs.

CHAPTER FOUR

# HOWELL MOUNTAIN

I n the northeastern slopes of the Napa Valley, rising above the low fogs that often settle along the valley floor, the vineyards on Howell Mountain often are blessed with several extra hours of sunlight, and the resulting grapes ripen to physiological maturity in a cool mountain climate. These wines show the same kind of stark beauty that you can see all around you in the area's wildly rugged landscape.

Visiting the small wineries on the back roads of Howell Mountain is a delightful way to spend a day in the wine country—and you might as well plan to spend the day. These are places well off the beaten path, and it can take half an hour or more to reach some of them after you leave the Silverado Trail. The best advice is to plan ahead and schedule two or three wine tasting appointments on the mountain and to bring up a picnic hamper. There are no restaurants up here, and both gourmet supplies and gasoline are limited in Angwin, the last little village on the route up the hillside.

# VIADER VINEYARD
# AND WINERY

1120 Deer Park Road ✦ Deer Park
St. Helena Highway (Highway 29) *to*
Deer Park Road/Sanitarium Road
*Tel:* 707.963.3816 ✦ www.viader.com

Tasting by appointment only

DELIA VIADER (PRONOUNCED VEE-AH-DARE) GREW UP IN FRANCE AS THE DAUGHTER OF A DIPLOMAT AND MIGHT never have become a winemaker at all, having completed a doctorate in philosophy at the Sorbonne and studied financial management at M.I.T. and the University of California at Berkeley. But she was a wine enthusiast—and, as a single mother, she wanted to raise her children in a place like Napa.

When she founded Viader in the mid-1980s, after the heyday of the 1970s and before the renaissance of the 1990s, there wasn't a lot of glamour in the California wine business, and there were only a handful of women working as *vignerons*. Delia started out making fewer than 1,500 cases a year. She came to the winemaking business with a global

perspective, and from the beginning her wines have found their place among the great vintages of the world. Today the winery—run by Delia with the help of son Alan and daughter Janet—produces around 7,000 cases annually, and her wines have been among the *Wine Spectator*'s Top 100 Wines on several occasions—including the number one spot on the publication's cover for the 1999 vintage.

Despite having earned a place on the world stage, this is a word-of-mouth winery. Delia makes wines, she says, for a global palate, and the proof is in the tasting.

The Viader wines aren't made in the style of the California "fruit bomb," where the rich fruit and berry flavors take precedence over some of a wine's more subtle structural elements. The estate is best known for its super-premium Viader cabernet sauvignon and cabernet franc blend ($90), although it also produces a clonal blend of syrah ($50). Under the "V" label there is an expressive petit verdot and cabernet sauvignon blend ($125), and the winery bottles as

"Dare" wines a changing line-up of more experimental releases—a tempranillo, a 100% cabernet franc, and a summer rosé wine that always sells out within a matter of weeks ($20–40).

The other winemakers in the valley will tell you that the view from the back deck of the tasting room at Viader is easily one of the most spectacular in all of Napa, and there are few spots anywhere more perfectly suited for watching the sunset over the hills of the wine country. The Mayacamas range and Mount St. Helena are spread out before you, the welcome is gracious, and the wines delicious no matter what time of the day you come. There are significant discounts for purchases on the futures program (30%). The fee for tasting is $35, waived with purchase.

# LADERA VINEYARDS

150 White Cottage Road South ✦ Angwin
St. Helena Highway (Highway 29) or the Silverado Trail to
Deer Park Road east until White Cottage Road
*Tel:* 707.965.2445 ✦ www.laderavineyards.com
Tasting by appointment only

**A**NGWIN IS A LONG WAY ABOVE THE VALLEY FLOOR, AND, IF YOU'RE PLANNING A VISIT TO THE FAMED HILLSIDE VINE-yards on Howell Mountain—Napa's first recognized sub-appellation—spending the day makes the most sense. There are more than a dozen small vintners clustered around White Cottage Road and Summit Lake Drive, and one you wouldn't want to miss is Ladera Vineyards. This mountain *terroir* was first planted to zinfandel as early as the 1870s, and the stone winery on the property dates back to the 1880s. The first proprietors delivered their grapes by carriage to Oakville, sending long-distance messages by lantern from nearby Sentinel Hill.

When owners Anne and Pat Stotesbery set about restoring the winery in early 2000, the old wood floors were re-milled and used as paneling in the open barn-style tasting room and production facility. To-

day, there are eighty-one acres of planted vineyards on the property, and the family business—run by Anne and Pat, with the help of three of their four children—produces a range of excellent wines, including the valley's only Howell Mountain-designate sauvignon blanc. There is also a Howell Mountain 100% merlot, a Howell Mountain cabernet, and one of the rare 100% malbec wines in California (prices from $25–70). Total production is around 12,000 cases annually.

Pat and Anne started out cattle ranching in Montana and came to wine country to pursue their passion for wines. Today, the winery has a wine club (members are invited to use the winery's *caves* for private dinners and special events) and a hands-on harvest experience for anyone hankering to experience his or her first crush. It's a chance to participate in one of the most festive times of the year and to get a deluxe behind-the-scenes look at what making premium wine is all about (prices from $1,200). There are also occasional twilight winery tours, where you can enjoy the beautiful gardens at dusk and soak up the atmosphere at one of the valley's most picturesque ghost wineries. The charge for tasting is $15; the tasting and complete winery tour is $25; the fee is often waived with a significant purchase of wine.

# LAMBORN FAMILY VINEYARDS

1984 Summit Lake Drive ✦ Angwin
St. Helena Highway (Highway 29) *to* Deer Park Road east,
left on White Cottage Road, left onto Summit Lake Drive
*Tel:* 925.254.0511 ✦ www.lamborn.com
Tours by appointment only

HERE IN NAPA, THERE ARE BACK LANE WINERIES, AND THEN THERE ARE BACK LANE WINERIES. IF YOU ARE LOOKING for the unfiltered experience of family winemaking—the kind of place where you stand on the summit of a mountain vineyard with the world at your feet and get your shoes muddy walking through the vines with a winegrower—then Lamborn should be at the top of your list. Perched high up on Napa's famed Howell Mountain, more than 2,000 feet above sea level, there are sweeping views of pine forests and distant canyons, where growers occasionally have to contend with the bears who stop by to eat the fruit off the vines at harvest.

Now in its third generation, the winery was founded in the early 1970s by the father-and-son team of Bob and Mike Lamborn, who started out selling grapes from the hillside property and making some garage wine that Mike admits was pretty dubious. But the fault was never with the grapes, and this is some of the most coveted *terroir* in the valley. By 1983, the family had released their first commercial vintage. In 1996, Heidi Barrett—the winemaker behind the super-cult vintages at Screaming Eagle—began crafting the Lamborn wines, and today, Mike and his wife Terry run the eight-acre

estate vineyards with sons Matt and Brian.

Mountain wines in the Napa Valley are known for their beautiful tannins, the combined result of cooler days and, here above the fog line, more hours of sunshine. The grapes ripen slowly. These aren't fruit bomb wines but vintages that will age beautifully, an increasingly rare thing in the wine country when it comes to zinfandel, which is one of the two wines in the Lamborn portfolio ($41). Of course, they also make a hillside cabernet ($115). These are the wines that made Napa famous, and with a total annual production of fewer than 2,000 cases, the Lamborn wines are in demand. But if you want to sample them, a visit to this mountaintop vineyard is your best bet. Bring a picnic if you like, a pair of good walking shoes, and all those agricultural questions you always wanted to ask a winegrower. Appointments need to be made several weeks in advance.

# SUMMIT LAKE
# VINEYARDS AND WINERY

2000 Summit Lake Drive ✦ Angwin

St. Helena Highway (Highway 29) *to* Deer Park Road east,
left on White Cottage Road, and left onto Summit Lake Drive

*Tel:* 707.965.2488 ✦ www.summitlakevineyards.com

Tasting by appointment only

F EW THINGS ARE MORE CHARACTERISTICALLY NAPA THAN SIPPING A GLASS OF SOMETHING SPECIAL OUT IN THE vineyards and dreaming a bit about what life might be like in the wine country. And there are few places more beautiful to do that bit of dreaming than up on the top of Howell Mountain. Among the places not to miss here far above the valley floor is Summit Lake Vineyards and Winery, which has been owned and operated by the Brakesman family since the early 1970s.

When the family bought the land, growing on it were some pre-Prohibition zinfandel vines that had been abandoned for more than thirty years, and the initial plan was to fix up the vineyards and flip the property. As it turns out, the Brakesmans never left. Family and friends helped to replant the vineyards, and by the late 1980s the estate was producing a couple of hundred cases of wine a year.

Today, production caps out at just over a thousand cases annually, and, in addition to a zinfandel and zinfandel port, there are small lots of hillside cabernet sauvignon and petite sirah (wines from $24–65). All the wines are named for grandchildren. This is a word-of-mouth kind of winery—the family doesn't submit their wines to contests and doesn't

advertise. Instead, the family encourages folks to educate their own palate, to discover what they like in a wine, and why. The wines produced here on Howell Mountain—some of the most coveted vineyard property in the valley—have expressive tannins and a unique minerality that's hard not to love.

On warm days tasting at Summit Lake takes place outside, where you can enjoy the views of Pope Valley and the Yolo Mountains in the distance. On rainy days, you'll gather around the kitchen table. If you're traveling with children, the barnyard ducks and farm animals will be an instant hit, and you're welcome to bring a picnic up from the valley if you're planning to spend the day up on the mountain. There's no charge for the tasting.

# BLACK SEARS ESTATE

2615 Summit Lake Drive ✦ Angwin

St. Helena Highway (Highway 29) to Deer Park Road east,
left on White Cottage Road, and left onto Summit Lake Drive

Tel: 707.963.1334 ✦ cell 707.889.1243 ✦ www.blacksears.com

Tours by appointment only

A PASSIONATE LOVE OF WINE LED JOYCE BLACK SEARS AND JERRE SEARS TO PURCHASE THIS RURAL PROPERTY UP ON Howell Mountain in 1980, and, without any fanfare or big advertising budget, they have been quietly making about 500 cases of mountain wines from some of the finest fruit raised in their vineyards. While most of the grapes are sold to prestige winemakers throughout the valley, Joyce and Jerre—along with their daughter Ashley and son-in-law Chris—reserve some of their annual crop to make a couple of wines each year under their own label. The idea behind estate wines is to make something that captures the essence of place, and that's the focus at Black Sears, where the flagship wines are a zinfandel ($42) and a cabernet sauvignon ($80), with all the intense tannins and complex aromas that have made this one of the most coveted appellations in Napa. They also occasionally release a Howell Mountain Red, a cabernet sauvignon, and a cabernet franc blend ($80).

Visits to the Howell Mountain estate are limited, and this remote location is beyond back lane. These are wines made amid some of the wine country's most rugged splendor, and they are categorically wines you are not going to find anywhere back home.

# BRAVANTE VINEYARDS

300 Stone Ridge Road ✦ Angwin
St. Helena Highway (Highway 29) or the
Silverado Trail *to* Deer Park Road east until
White Cottage Road, left on Stone Ridge Road
*Tel:* 707.972.1114 ✦ www.bravantewine.com
Tasting by appointment only

**A**S A YOUNG COUPLE, GEORGE AND NANCY BRAVANTE LIVED UP HERE ON HOWELL MOUNTAIN IN THE PALE YELLOW ranch house that today is part of the hospitality area for Bravante Vineyards, and the feeling that there are real people and a real family behind this small winery is one of the charms of a visit to the estate in the hills above the Napa Valley floor. Today, the ranch house is used for picnics, parties, and private events (and there are few places in the wine country that would make a more perfect venue for a special occasion), and tasting takes place down in the winery or caves, which are a delightful retreat on a hot summer afternoon. There are also spectacular valley views from the property, and if you are spending the day up on Howell Mountain, you can pick up a picnic lunch in the morning and take advantage of them from the lawn or picnic tables. The winery is great for groups, you're welcome to bring picnic baskets, and even well-behaved dogs are welcome to join your party.

Of course, you'll need a bottle of the Bravante family wine to go with that picnic, and there are plenty of delicious options. The family makes around 3,000 cases of wine a year. The estate red wines ($40–60), grown either on this property or in a vineyard just a bit further up the hillside, are mostly Bordeaux varietals, emphasizing cabernet sauvignon, cabernet franc, merlot, and several blends. There is also a sauvignon blanc/ sauvignon musque blend ($20), made from fruit sourced in the Suisun Valley—the emerging wine country between San Francisco and Sacramento. The tasting is $10, waived with purchase.

# CLARK-CLAUDON VINEYARDS

P.O. Box 15 ✦ St. Helena

Tasting off site, call for details

*Tel:* 707.965.9393 ✦ www.clarkclaudon.com

Tasting by appointment only

**L**AND COSTS A FORTUNE IN THE NAPA VALLEY, SO IT TAKES SOME SPECIAL MAGIC FOR A YOUNG COUPLE TO BE ABLE to purchase 154 acres of hillside property on Howell Mountain. When Laurie Clark-Claudon tells the story of how she and her husband Tom were able to make a life for themselves in the wine country, she puts it down to hard work, a willingness to take a risk, serendipity, and the kindness of strangers.

In the 1980s, Tom started his own vineyard management company and was tending the grapes for prestigious clients like Spottswoode and St. Supéry, while Laurie worked as a schoolteacher and then psychother-

apic[...] When a friend told them about a property for sale up in the hills above the Napa Valley, they went to have a look and fell in love with the place, but the price was completely beyond their reach. To their astonishment, the owner worked with them over a period of years to make sure they could buy it.

Today, this special piece of the wine country is home to the Clark-Claudon Estate vineyards, where their estate cabernet sauvignon wines are born. The vineyards are run by Tom and Laurie, their children Briana and Josh, and their spouses, and occasionally assisted, of course, by the young third generation, who are learning to pick leaves out of the bins at harvest. Wine tasting ($20, waived with purchase) takes place in a small cottage, where the views from the deck take in the vineyards and creek and the forest beyond, and guests settle in with wine and cheese to savor the mountain views here at nearly a thousand feet above the valley floor.

There are eighteen acres planted to vineyards, and the property is a natural oasis for bears, coyote, birds, and even the occasional mountain lion. The Clark-Claudon Wild Iris sauvignon blanc ($26), made with fruit from vineyards farmed by Josh and his company, Clark Vineyard Management, is named for the flowers that grow at the edge of the estate vineyard. The label of their estate cabernet sauvignon ($78), an elegant wine with luscious mountain tannins, features the winery's signature feathers, a nod to the wildlife that surrounds them here on Howell Mountain. Occasionally a wine is made from the thousand vines planted around the family home, released under their Eternity label. These are small-production lots (under 1,500 cases) from one of Napa's most prestigious appellations, and those who know the Clark-Claudon wines won't be surprised to learn that, since their first release in 1993, they have received scores in the 90s for every single vintage produced.

# SAUNTER

P.O. Box 637 ✦ St. Helena
Tasting off site, call for information
*Tel:* 707.963.8695 ✦ www.saunterwines.com
Tasting by appointment only

NYONE WHO HAS BEEN IN THE WINEMAKING BUSINESS FOR LONG KNOWS THAT GROWING GRAPES TAKES BEING A GOOD farmer, and many of Napa's small family winemakers got their start out in the vineyards, where they learned the art and craft of a great wine from the ground up. That's the story behind one of the valley's newest and smallest boutique labels, Saunter. The shared vision of the young husband-and-wife team of Joshua and Heather Clark, Saunter released its first vintage in 2008—just 190 cases.

Heather, who grew up on a sunflower and wheat farm in eastern Colorado, came to Napa after college, drawn to the wine industry. She and Josh married in 2006. He runs the vineyard management company that his father founded, and Saunter is the result of their shared passion for wine and winemaking. The small production of estate cabernet sauvignon ($90) comes from the Clark-Claudon family vineyards up on Howell Mountain, and the petite sirah wine ($45) is sourced from grapes grown a bit further up-valley in Calistoga. There is no charge for the winemaker's tour, which is al fresco–style up in the vineyards, and the couple is happy to arrange barrel tasting for visitors interested in learning not just how a great wine is crafted, but how it develops.

# SPRING MOUNTAIN

L ocated up in the steep hills that rise above the western floor of the Napa Valley and connect California's most celebrated wine country with its prestigious neighbor in Sonoma, the Spring Mountain District is one of the most beautiful parts of a beautiful place. The thirty-odd wineries in the appellation are mostly strung out along Spring Mountain Road, which twists and turns its way dramatically through small wooded canyons up to a high natural pass. The road then begins its descent into Sonoma County.

The Spring Mountain District has only about a thousand acres of vineyards, and this is a place where few tourists come. But the tasting experiences on the mountain—where small family wineries and hand-tilled vineyards are the norm—are wonderfully intimate, and the wines from the appellation are among the world's most coveted. Because of the distance from the main tasting route, this is a place to plan to spend a day, bringing along an al fresco luncheon or making plans for a catered meal at one of the wineries.

# MARSTON FAMILY VINEYARD

P.O. Box 668 ✦ St. Helena
Tasting off site, call for details
*Tel.* 707.963.8490 ✦ www.marstonfamilyvineyard.com
Tasting by appointment only

SOMETIMES IN THE WINE COUNTRY THERE ARE PLACES SO BEAUTIFUL THAT YOU CAN'T QUITE BELIEVE YOU'VE stumbled upon them, and among all my Napa Valley picks—and there are some stunningly wonderful places—the Marston Family Vineyard is right at the very top of the charts. These are great wines, created in the midst of splendor and history, and made by some of the nicest people you'll ever meet.

It's a long and winding drive up to the estate, past hot springs and riverbeds and redwood forests, and then you'll turn up a small track where the view opens onto hillside vineyards and distant views of tree-covered mountain slopes. Of the original five hundred acres that the Marston family purchased back in the 1960s as a summer retreat, almost half have been donated to the Napa Valley Land Conservation trust, an organization devoted to preserving the wild rural spaces of the wine country. The result is a woodland oasis, where wild turkeys meander through the vineyards and where you feel a thousand miles away from the frantic tourist pace of St. Helena on a summer day.

At 1,100 feet, these steep hillside vineyards produce the rich mountain tannins that have made the Napa Valley famous. Winemakers here use gentle barrel fermentation to tame those tannins without jeopardizing the complex layering of the gorgeous fruits. Of the fifty acres of vineyards on the property, the oldest were planted back in the 1920s using horse and plow, and while there are a few historic blocks, most of the family's vineyards were replanted in the 1990s to cabernet sauvignon, merlot, and syrah. The largest part of the vineyards is under contract with Beringer, which has used the fruit for its acclaimed private reserve wines for more than twenty years.

Until that contract expires, the Marston family will produce just a few hundred cases of wine a year. And the Marstons make just one wine—a terrific 100% cabernet sauvignon ($100) that *Wine News* has ranked as its number one publisher's pick and awarded a stellar 96 points. *Wine Spectator* and Robert Parker have both ranked recent vintages in the 90s, as well.

Three generations of Marstons run the family winery—parents John and Elizabeth, children Elizabeth and John, and a senior generation of Marston grandparents. The tasting room is a vintage tin-roofed hay barn, once the site of an old ghost winery on the property, with the feel of a 1920s New England summer camp. One of the property's many natural springs bubbles up in the courtyard, and just beyond you can see the old track of the original stagecoach road that once ran past the barn and connected this most southerly end of Spring Mountain to the higher elevations and then to Sonoma County on the far side of the valley. When you visit, be sure to ask to see the sign that Clark Gable—who spent his honeymoon in the cottage on the property—once used for target practice, and make sure you also learn about the Marston second label, E.J. It's a small project that the younger Elizabeth and John have recently started, representing the best in the next generation of Napa winemaking.

# ROBERT KEENAN WINERY

3660 Spring Mountain Road ✦ St. Helena

St. Helena Highway (Highway 29) *to* Madrona Avenue,
right onto Spring Mountain Road

*Tel:* 707.963.9177 ✦ www.keenanwinery.com

Tasting by appointment only

**S**PRING MOUNTAIN IS ONE OF NAPA VALLEY'S MOST SCENIC APPELLATIONS, AND, ALTHOUGH THIS AVA HAS BEEN MAKing some of America's most acclaimed wines for decades, visitors to the wine country have only recently discovered the scenic tasting rooms tucked away here in the hills that separate Napa from nearby Sonoma County. One of the pioneers in making world-class wines on Spring Mountain is Robert Keenan Wines, founded

on the site of an old nineteenth-century ghost winery in the 1970s by Robert Keenan and still run today by his son, Michael.

For Robert Keenan, a life in the wine business was the natural outgrowth of his passion for the history of the great French châteaux—and his gift for real estate investment. Because his maternal grandfather was also an avid collector of fine French wines, Michael grew up appreciating great vintages. Today the winery produces some great vintages of its own. This was one of *Wine and Spirit*'s top 100 wineries of the year in 2006, and, since 2001, thirty-three of its wines have received scores of 90 points or more from Robert Parker, including the 94-point 2005 reserve Mernet—Michael's signature 50-50 blend of merlot and cabernet. Among the white wines, there is a standout summer blend of chardonnay, viognier, and marsanne, and, Michael will tell you with a laugh, "we also do a non-malolactic chardonnay, so it actually doesn't suck." It's an impressive record for a fifty-acre estate whose total annual production is under 15,000 cases a year.

Unusually in the valley, the family was able to restore the original Italian hill-style winery, and the drive up Spring Mountain road is easily one of the most beautiful rural routes in the wine country. Most wines are in the $25–100 range, and there is no charge for tasting appointments.

# TERRA VALENTINE

3787 Spring Mountain Road ✦ St. Helena
St. Helena Highway (Highway 29) *to* Madrona Avenue,
right onto Spring Mountain Road
*Tel.* 707.967.8340 ✦ www.terravalentine.com
Tasting by appointment only

HEN ANGUS AND MARGARET WURTELE BOUGHT THIS
VINEYARD ESTATE ON SPRING MOUNTAIN IN THE 1990s,
it might as well have been Sleeping Beauty's castle.
Originally built in the 1970s as the site of the Yverdon
Winery, the vineyards had been torn out and the building
shuttered for more than a decade. The hillside terrain was so overgrown
that it meant hacking a pathway to the doorstep.

Today, renamed Terra Valentine—a nod to Angus's father, who was
born on February 14 and built a commercial empire in the varnish business—the estate looks every bit the fairytale retreat. Perched two thousand feet above the valley floor, amid great natural beauty, the château-
style stone winery is illuminated with stained glass windows, depicting
themes of classical literature and wine. The deluxe one-and-a-half-hour
tasting appointment (starting at $30), which focuses on wine education
and pairs the Terra Valentine wines with artisanal cheeses and dark
chocolate, takes place under the watchful eye of St. Geneviève, the pa-
tron saint of Paris, in a room decorated with eighteenth-century English oak panels originally destined for the Hearst Castle in San Simeon.
There is also a more casual opportunity to taste wines out on the balcony,
where you can soak in the sunshine and admire the views ($20).

The winery has two estate vineyards, one here on the property and one a bit further down the mountain, and the real emphasis is on cabernet sauvignon wines. There is also a dry Alsatian-style estate Riesling, an unfiltered French-style pinot noir, and a full-bodied Bordeaux blend (most wines from $30–85). Tasting fees are applied to purchase.

# CHARBAY WINERY AND DISTILLERY

4001 Spring Mountain Road ✦ St. Helena
St. Helena Highway (Highway 29) *to* Madrona Avenue,
right onto Spring Mountain Road
*Tel:* 707.963.9327 ✦ www.charbay.com
Tasting Tuesday *to* Saturday 10AM *to* 4PM, by appointment only

R UN BY MILES AND SUSAN KARAKASEVIC AND THEIR SON MARKO, CHARBAY HAS A REPUTATION AS ONE OF THE finest producers of boutique spirits in the country, and outside their Napa Valley production facility you can get what might be your first look at a pot still. Theirs originally came from Cognac, France. Miles is from Serbia and is a twelfth-generation distiller. *Spirit Journal* has ranked Charbay's vodka the best in the world for several years running, and the distillery's limited-release whiskey ($325) is a runaway cult favorite.

What fewer people know is that the family has been making wines, brandy, and aperitifs up on their Spring Mountain estate—at 2,300 feet above sea level, the highest tasting bar in the county—for more than twenty-five years. They produce almost a dozen different wines, including around sixty cases a year of chardonnay, maybe a hundred cases of dry rosé, and of course a 100% cabernet sauvignon wine made from fruit grown in Oakville (wines from $25–50). You'll also find a range of ports, fruit wines, and wine-based aperitifs. Poured over ice, these aperitifs are perfect summer afternoon cocktails. It's a family joke that, here at Charbay, no fruit is safe.

The tasting room is set along a rural back road above the Napa Valley, and in the winter months, when the still is running, it's a cozy and relaxed place to try something just a little bit different. Visitors gather around the bar in a winery filled with the scent of wood barrels to sample the wines, ports, and aperitifs; on Friday and Saturday there are barrel-tasting opportunities with Miles and Marko. Midweek there's an al fresco port and cigar pairing. Tasting fees are $20. And, while California law won't allow you to taste any of the stronger stuff here at the tasting room, the family offers a terrific seminar on the art of distilling, taught by folks who are unquestionably masters ($40).

# SMITH-MADRONE
# VINEYARDS AND WINERY

4022 Spring Mountain Road
St. Helena Highway (Highway 29) & Madrona Avenue,
right on Spring Mountain Road
Tel: 707.963.2283 ✦ www.smithmadrone.com
Tasting by appointment only

THE ESTATE VINEYARDS AT SMITH-MADRONE BEAR THE TRACES OF THE HISTORY OF THE WINE COUNTRY. CHINESE workers first cleared the property in the middle of the nineteenth century, and parts of the ranch had been planted to vineyards more than a century ago. Today, visitors can also still see rows of old olive trees—and abundant evidence of the madrone trees that make up the second part of the name the Smith family have given to their hillside winery.

Stuart Smith founded the current winery in 1971, and the vineyards were planted a decade later by Stu and his brother Charles. Today, the two still run the winery, with Stu acting as general manager and Charles as the winemaker. The family's focus is on making a signature "old-fashioned Napa Valley kick-ass" cabernet sauvignon that was praised in *The New York Times* as a "lovely, structured" wine and recently tapped as one of the top hundred wines of 2007 by the *San Francisco Chronicle*. There are two white wines made on the property—a chardonnay and a riesling. The wines are under $40, and there is no charge for the tasting here at this mountain-top family vineyard, which is always led by one of the Smith brothers.

# PRIDE MOUNTAIN VINEYARDS

4026 Spring Mountain Road ✦ St. Helena

St. Helena Highway (Highway 29) *to* Madrona Avenue,

right on Spring Mountain Road; entrance a half-mile

past the Sonoma County line

*Tel:* 707.963.4949 ✦ www.pridewines.com

Tasting by appointment only, closed Tuesday and Sunday

HE OLD STAGECOACH ROAD FROM ST. HELENA TO SANTA
ROSA ONCE RAN ACROSS SPRING MOUNTAIN IN THE DAYS
before there was a county line separating Sonoma on the west
from Napa on the east. Down in the Pride Mountain vineyards,
the ruins of an old stone arch still mark the route of this first

wine-country highway, and today, the county line runs right through the middle of the family estate. In fact, in order to meet the strict regulations that govern the production and appellation of wines in Northern California, the Pride family spends some of their time during the crush moving equipment from one side of that line to the other.

What this means is that, perhaps uniquely, Pride produces both Sonoma and Napa wines made from a single ranch, and, if you ever wanted to learn about the complex intersection of *terroir* and appellation in winemaking, there is no better place to get a firsthand introduction. There is also no better place to learn about the world-class wines both counties have to offer. The Pride wines have made the *Wine Spectator*'s top 100 wines list on five occasions—including the 2005 Reserve Cabernet Sauvignon—and Robert Parker has tapped the winery as one of the top in the world.

When the family bought the ranch back in 1989, the first "tasting room" was a board between two barrels. Now, visitors gather around a pewter bar in an art-filled foyer, where the atmosphere is friendly and welcoming. The fee for a bar-side tasting is $5 per person. If at all possible, get a spot at the 10AM tasting—it's the only appointment of the day that includes the free vineyard tour, which includes a walk through the caves. You are also welcome to stop off on your own at the nineteenth-century stone ruins of the old Summit Winery, located on Pride Mountain property. Legend has it the winery was burned during prohibition for the insurance money, and it's a hauntingly picturesque spot.

If you're touring the wine country with more than a few friends, there is also a private tasting room seating up to a dozen people, where you can sit down for a more focused and educational experience ($15). Pride also offers a very exclusive private tasting in the caves, for special occasions ($75).

Owned and operated by the brother-and-sister team of Steve and Suzanne, and with founder and mother Carolyn still taking an interest, Pride is renowned for its signature cabernet sauvignon wines and produces excellent wines from other varietals grown on the property, including merlot, sangiovese, chardonnay, viognier, syrah, and a very small production dessert wine, Mistelle de Viognier. Prices range from $37–125, with most wines in the $55 range.

# BARNETT VINEYARDS

4070 Spring Mountain Road ✦ St. Helena
St. Helena Highway (Highway 29) *to* Madrona Avenue,
right onto Spring Mountain Road
*Tel.* 707.963.7075 ✦ www.barnettvineyards.com
Tasting by appointment only

THE HILLTOP SPANISH-STYLE ESTATE THAT IS HOME TO BARNETT VINEYARDS IS ONE OF THOSE SPECIAL PLACES IN the area where the natural beauty of everything that surrounds you is achingly lovely. On cool mornings, the fog crawls along the valley floor two thousand feet below, and there is a sense up here among the forests and the vineyards that you have entered some different, more magical world. Wine tasting at Barnett Vineyards starts

with a cave tour and a chance to try its acclaimed chardonnay and pinot noir offerings. On most days, tasting ends on the elevated deck, enjoying samples of the merlot and cabernet sauvignon wines that have made Barnett Vineyards one of the most celebrated small wineries in Napa Valley. There is also a sauvignon blanc and a rosé, both available only in the tasting room.

Established in 1989 by Fiona and Hal Barnett, who came to the wine country from San Francisco, Barnett Vineyards today produces around 7,000 cases of wine a year. The focus here is on crafting consistently excellent single-vineyard-designate wines, and these are wines the critics love. *Wine Enthusiast* rated Barnett's 2005 Rattlesnake Hill cabernet sauvignon ($125) a lofty 95 points, and scores in the 90s are typical for Bar-

nett Hill releases year after year. There are also several wines priced at the entry level if you're not yet a serious collector. Winemaker David Tate makes a superb and well-priced Anderson Valley pinot noir that sells out each year ($55), and there are several excellent wines starting at $25.

If you want to understand why Napa Valley has a reputation for world-class wines—and, in the bargain, you want to see some of the most gorgeous scenery going—Barnett Vineyards is a must. There are tours of the working winery and a chance to taste these small-production wines in an intimate and friendly setting. The fee for tasting is $25, which is waived with purchase unless you are part of a large group.

# BEHRENS FAMILY WINERY

4078 Spring Mountain Road ✦ St. Helena
St. Helena Highway (Highway 29) to Madrona Avenue,
right onto Spring Mountain Road
*Tel:* 707.963.1774 ✦ www.behrensfamilywinery.com
Tasting by appointment only

LES BEHRENS AND LISA DRINKWARD STARTED MAKING WINES UP IN CALIFORNIA'S NORTHERN HUMBOLDT COUNTY BACK in the early 1990s, when they had the idea to buy some grapes and make some house wine to serve at the award-winning restaurant they owned and ran. When it turned out they had a knack for making great wines, they found themselves with a growing project, and, before too long, with a dilemma. They realized they would have to either run a restaurant or run a winery, because there just weren't enough hours in a day to do both.

So the winery was born. In 1997 they sold the restaurant, and the next year, with partner Bob Hitchcock, they purchased a piece of hilltop winery property in Napa's Spring Mountain District. Although Bob retired back in 2004, Les and Lisa still make about 500 cases a year under the Behrens & Hitchcock label, but today the majority of their 3,000 cases a year are produced under the name Erna Schein Wines. There have been stellar accolades all around—*Food & Wine* has called it the year's top syrah, *Sunset* magazine the year's best red, and there have been rave reviews from Robert Parker. But Les will tell you that it's actually all about a winemaker putting heart and soul in a bottle. That's what you can taste in a really great wine.

The California wine country is filled with gorgeous views and natural beauty that will sometimes leave you breathless, but these little wineries up on Spring Mountain are some of Napa's most stunning. In the afternoons, there is a luminous quality to the atmosphere and long views over forested valleys. Tasting at Behrens Family Winery takes place amid all this splendor, in a vintage, wood-paneled Westcraft trailer, where there are quirky old postcards with scenes of the wine country and a window view.

Apart from tasting the Erna Schein and Behrens & Hitchcock releases, there are plenty of other wines to try here as well. The tasting room is essentially a five-in-one cooperative, and you can also discover the wines of Drinkward-Peschon, made as part of the collaboration between Lisa and Françoise Peschon. The two make around 500 cases a year of cabernet sauvignon under the Entre Deux Mères label. The winery's general manager, Schatzi Throckmorton, and her winemaker husband, Michael Hirby, make pinot noir and other wines here as well under the Relic Wines label; a recent assistant winemaker, Mark Porembski, makes a couple of hundred cases of wine called Zeitgeist, and Lisa's brother Rob-

ert Nenow released a small production under his name.

The focus in all the family projects is on red wines, mostly cabernet sauvignon, petite sirah, and merlot, although they also make the occasional rosé. The annual production changes, depending on what nature provides. The wines range from $40–85 and there is no charge for the hour-and-a-half tasting and tour of their working winery. If you happen to be in the wine country during the harvest, this is one of the few places where visitors are welcome to come watch the crush. For anyone who thinks that Napa is all glitz and glitter, this is the other side of the county—the kind of place where the pace is relaxed, the people are friendly, and the real work of making wine is the only thing on display.

# FISHER VINEYARDS

6200 St. Helena Road ✦ Santa Rosa
St. Helena Highway (Highway 29) *to* Madrona Avenue,
right onto Spring Mountain Road
*Tel:* 707.539.7511 ✦ www.fishervineyards.com
Tasting by appointment only

**F**RED AND JUELLE FISHER BOUGHT THEIR FIRST HUNDRED
ACRES OF VINEYARD PROPERTY UP ON SPRING MOUNTAIN
in 1973, and today they produce 5,000 cases of handcrafted
wines with both Sonoma County and Napa Valley appellations.
While the Spring Mountain tasting room is technically on the

western Sonoma side of the county line that runs through the Mayacamas range, the family also farms seventy acres of land along the storied Silverado Trail.

Their children grew up in these vineyards on both sides of the county line, and today the winery is a two-generation family affair, with all three of the children involved in daily operations. From the Spring Mountain tasting room, there are views in both directions, as far as the Sonoma Coast to the west and Knights Valley to the east, and the terraced vineyards glow golden in the late afternoon sun up here in the mountain *terroir*. The wood for the winery was milled from redwood trees and fir on the property, and in the warmer months tasting takes place outdoors, where there's a wood-fired pizza oven. There aren't any restaurants up on Spring Mountain, and if you're looking to work a lunch into your tasting itinerary, gourmet spreads can be included as part of a visit (prices starting at $60).

The winemaker's tour and tasting includes a walk through the vineyards, a trip through the cellars and the working winery, and, of course, the chance to sample some of these premium wines. The Fisher family produces both Sonoma County and Napa Valley single-vineyard-designate cabernet sauvignon wines, a range of Bordeaux-style red wine that includes a Napa Valley merlot and cabernet franc blend, and syrah and chardonnay wines made from grapes on the Spring Mountain estate. The Napa Valley cabernet from the Lamb Vineyard has consistently scored points in the 90s from the *Wine Advocate*, and the 1997 Wedding Vineyard cabernet—described as "potentially perfect" and a "modern-day California legend"—is, at 99 points, one of highest ranking American cabernets ever made. The fee for tasting is $40, waived with the purchase of three or more bottles.

# CHAPTER SIX

# DOWNTOWN ST. HELENA

The small city of St. Helena arguably is the cultural heart of the Napa wine country, and Highway 29 runs right through the middle of its quaint—and often congested—little Main Street. At the peak of the tourist season, driving through downtown St. Helena is an exercise in patience, and perhaps this is the best reason of all to pull over, breathe deeply, and spend a bit of time exploring the area. Here you will find high-end boutiques, art galleries, antique stores, and any number of excellent bistros, restaurants, and wine bars, and it is easy to while away an hour or two in the afternoon wandering the streets and shops. In the morning, before you hit the tasting trail, St. Helena also has several excellent bakeries and cafés, where you can pick up a pastry and a steaming latte on your way to your first appointment. There are many small family wineries tucked in along St. Helena's residential back streets and on the outskirts of the city.

# SALVESTRIN WINERY

397 Main Street ✦ St. Helena
South of St. Helena on the west side of Highway 29;
look for the white arches
*Tel.* 707.963.5105 ✦ www.salvestrinwinery.com
Tasting by appointment only

WHEN YOU'RE PLANNING YOUR DAY ON THE TASTING TRAIL, SALVESTRIN WINERY IS ONE OF THOSE PLACES where you want to leave yourself a bit of extra time. The people here are so congenial that you are bound to get chatting, and it would be a shame to have to cut short something quite so pleasant.

What's hard to believe sometimes is that this charming winery—which has nothing of Napa commercial glitz about it—is hidden right in plain sight, only a few minutes from downtown St. Helena. When you arrive, Salvestrin Winery feels just like what it is: a small family business and a labor of love. The family has been farming this property since 1932, when John and Emma Salvestrin bought it from its first recorded owner, the renowned Napa Valley viticulturalist Dr. George Crane. Today, three successive generations of the Salvestrin family are part of the story—Eddie and Susanne, their son Rich and his wife Shannon, and their young girls, Tessa, Emma, and Hannah. The senior Salvestrins live in a sprawling Victorian home next to the vineyards and tasting room, and you're likely to meet the big red cat and the two family dogs in the yard.

While the family has been growing grapes here for more than seventy-

five years, they didn't start commercially producing their own wines until the mid-1990s, and the winery only opened in 2001. They still sell about half of their grapes to other winemakers in the valley. With the rest, they produce around 3,500 cases a year of traditional Italian-style wines and Bordeaux varietals. Coming down the lane to the winery, you drive past their old-vine sangiovese plantings. Further back in the vineyards is some zinfandel that was planted more than a hundred years back.

If you've always wondered about the significance of old-vine plantings or wanted to ask a winemaker about the history of viticulture in the Napa Valley, there's no better chance. On warm afternoons, wine tasting often starts with a glass of sauvignon blanc ($22 per bottle) on the picnic tables outside the family's small winery, overlooking the vineyards and surrounded by fruit trees. Then, upstairs in the barn, there's a chance to try some of the Salvestrin reds. The estate makes a cabernet sauvignon, a petite sirah, a 100% sangiovese, a reserve cabernet sauvignon, and a

signature heritage Italian blend. Called Retaggio, it's a blend of sangiovese, merlot, cabernet sauvignon, and petite sirah. The wines range from $22–110, with most around $40, and many are available only in the tasting room or from their allocation list.

The fee for tasting is $15, and you're welcome to bring a picnic. Or, with advance notice, Rich's mom Susanne, a fabulous cook, can fix you a gourmet luncheon ($50 per person, includes the wine tasting) or help you arrange to have a special event at the winery.

# ARGER-MARTUCCI VINEYARDS

1455 Inglewood Avenue ✦ St. Helena

Highway 29 *to* Inglewood Avenue west

*Tel* 707.963.4334 ✦ www.arger-martucci.com

Tasting daily 10AM *to* 5PM, barrel tasting by appointment

THIS FAMILY WINERY HAS ITS ROOTS IN A WINE-COUNTRY WEEKEND. BACK IN 1975, WHEN JULIE AND KOSTA ARGER were on their honeymoon in Napa, they happened to stop by Heitz Cellars to sample some wines. They hit it off immediately with proprietors Joe and Alice Heitz, and the next year the couple returned to work the harvest. For Kosta, who was beginning his first year in medical school, this was the beginning of a passionate

enthusiasm for wine and winemaking. That year, he made his first home wines, and today his son Anthony still remembers fondly their long drives back up to Napa each autumn, where they picked up the grapes that the family would press out in the garage.

And for more than twenty years, the Arger family wines were really just that: home wines. Kosta pursued his career as a cardiologist in Reno, Nevada, all the while dreaming of Napa. That all changed in 1997, when the Arger family purchased some forty-odd acres of property on Atlas Peak. In 1998, they partnered with their friends Rich and Carol Martucci, and today it's still a family affair. Kosta continues to practice medicine in Reno, but his weekends are in the wine country. Rich manages the operations, assisted by respective sons Anthony Arger and Vincent Martucci.

One of Napa's up-and-coming appellations, the Atlas Peak AVA on the western slopes of the Vaca mountain range is turning out some high-quality cabernet sauvignon and cabernet franc, and at 1,350 feet the Arger-Martucci vineyards produce fruit that ripens slowly with the longer hours of sunlight and cooler temperatures of the high valleys. The families produce around 5,000 cases of wine a year (ranging from $20–100), including an award-winning syrah, cabernet sauvignon, cabernet franc wines, petite sirah, a proprietary red, and white blends. They also produce a special dessert wine blended from Semillon and sauvignon blanc, and rosé fans will be delighted to discover their dry *saigniée sauvage*, which you could drink all day at $20 a bottle.

The fee for tasting is $15, and this is one of the relatively few small wineries in the Napa Valley where you don't need an appointment to come visit. Just look for the old red barn as you are coming down Inglewood, and you'll spot the vineyards out front. In back, by the tasting room, there are rose gardens and a cool poolside spot and, of course, a warm welcome.

# SPOTTSWOODE ESTATE
# VINEYARD AND WINERY

1902 Madrona Avenue ✦ St. Helena

St. Helena Highway (Highway 29) *to* Madrona Avenue

*Tel:* 707.963.0134 ✦ www.spottswoode.com

Tasting Tuesday and Friday at 10AM by appointment only

HEN JACK AND MARY NOVAK MOVED THEIR FAMILY TO THE NAPA VALLEY IN 1972, LAND WAS STILL $2,000 an acre and grapes sold at the co-op for a couple of hundred dollars a ton. The plan was to drive a tractor, grow grapes, and maybe make some wine. Jack was a physician, and it seemed like an idyllic place to raise their five children.

But, as is the way in the wine country, after replanting forty acres of old pre-Prohibition vineyards to zinfandel, sauvignon blanc, and cabernet sauvignon and taking classes in viniculture, the family produced, despite Jack's untimely death in 1977, its first vintage of cabernet sauvignon in 1982. Today Spottswoode, named after the historic 1882 Victorian estate and forty-six-acre property that is still the

family home, makes, under the stewardship of daughters Beth and Lindy, around 6,000 cases a year of acclaimed cabernet sauvignon and sauvignon blanc wines, the former produced entirely from grapes grown in their organically farmed estate vineyard. Robert Parker called the recently released 2005 Spottswoode estate cabernet a "beauty" and gave it 96 points—but then, points in the 90s and accolades are nothing new at Spottswoode, where the emphasis is on creating world-class wines that will cellar beautifully.

While this land was once all farms, today the winery is located in the midst of a residential section against the mountains on the west side of St. Helena, and tasting takes place at a long wooden table in a cheerful ranch house overlooking the historic nineteenth-century stone barn winery that serves as a barrel room and production facility. Wines range from around $36–130; there is no charge for tours and tasting.

# ANOMALY VINEYARDS

455 Bella Vista Court ✦ St. Helena
St. Helena Highway (Highway 29) *to* Grayson Avenue,
south on Crane Avenue, west on Vallejo Street *to* Bella Vista Court
*Tel.* 707.967.8448 ✦ www.anomalyvineyards.com
Tasting by appointment only

**S**TEVE AND LINDA GOLDFARB FIRST CAME TO NAPA LOOKING FOR A SMALL WEEKEND PLACE WHERE THEY COULD retreat from their busy life in San Francisco as a lawyer and paralegal. In 1997, they came to the wine country on Linda's birthday and fell in love with a house that happened to come with six rows of grape vines. They moved in over the summer, and, come fall, there were grapes to be picked. The couple went at it with kitchen shears, and eventually their neighbor, a grape grower, took pity on them and suggested hiring some seasoned pickers to help with the small harvest. Using information from every book they could read on home winemaking, Steve and Linda crushed the grapes in their garage and ultimately made thirty cases of wine using a barrel they bought from the folks over at Cakebread Cellars.

Their foray into the winemaking business might have ended there if Linda hadn't happened to be on the board of the local animal shelter. While the wine Steve and Linda made sat in bottles in their garage, Linda worked on the shelter's fundraiser, which included a wine auction. She asked one of the sponsors to put their wine into a blind tasting to see if it was even drinkable. The tasting panel called them the following week and said, "You need to make more of this wine; it's fantastic." And

that was how Anomaly Vineyards got its start.

Their first vintage in 1997 was released only to friends. Three years later they hired a winemaker and started commercially producing wines. A new winery soon followed. Anomaly still makes only one wine—a cabernet sauvignon blended with a small amount of petit verdot and cabernet franc ($85). Their vintages consistently receive high praise, but the motto they go by is printed on their cork: "Trust Your Palate."

From the Tuscan-style fieldstone winery, there are impressive views of the Mayacamas Mountains. Tasting appointments take place in the cozy underground cellar. Anomaly also sells a cold-pressed extra-virgin olive oil ($30) imported from Cortona, Italy, where Steve's brother and sister-in-law own a small home on a property with olive orchards; the oils are the fruits of that good fortune. And why is the wine named Anomaly? Steve and Linda will tell you cheerfully that "anomaly" means unusual and unexpected, and "that's us doing this!"

# S. F. CHASE FAMILY CELLARS

P.O. Box 508 ✦ St. Helena

Tasting off site, call for directions

*Tel.* 707.963.1284 ✦ www.chasecellars.com

Tasting by appointment only

THIS SMALL FAMILY VINEYARD, RUN BY PAM SIMPSON WITH THE HELP OF BROTHER JEFF BLAUM, IS NAMED AFTER THE nineteenth-century rancher Sarah Esther Chase, whose family founded the original Greystone Cellars, today the home of the Culinary Institute of America. Her children planted in 1903 some of the zinfandel vines that descendants still farm today. Here on this old creek bed, the roots of these dry-farmed plants reach down more than thirty feet to find water, and the result is wine with ripe dark fruits and a large finish.

Chase Family Cellars currently produces fewer than 2,000 cases a year of wine, including an old-vine reserve zinfandel, a petite sirah, a cabernet sauvignon, and a zinfandel port-style wine, made with the locally produced Charbay brandy (wines from $45–75). The estate also releases around eighty cases a year of a dry rosé. Readers of *Food & Wine* will have seen the wine featured on the cover of the November 2007 Thanksgiving issue; these are wines that pair well with food. There is no charge for tasting.

# ANDREW LANE WINES

1410 62nd Street ✦ Emeryville

Tasting off site, call for directions

*Tel.* 510.526.4930 ✦ www.andrewlanewines.com

Tasting by appointment only

**A**T ANDREW LANE, WINEMAKER AND WINE EDUCATOR DREW DICKSON OFFERS INTIMATE INTRODUCTIONS TO THE ART of winemaking in the Napa Valley and exclusive autumn events celebrating the arrival of their beaujolais-nouveau-inspired wines. As the sons of winemaker David Dickson, who established the winery back in 1978, brothers Drew and Lane grew up here in the wine country. Today, the family produces around 1,700 cases a year of premium wines, focusing on cabernet franc, cabernet sauvignon, petite sirah, merlot, and an innovative gamay noir (most wines $20–50). There is a particularly nice Mediterranean blend that balances sangiovese, zinfandel, and petite sirah. Their 2005 cabernet franc was ranked best in the valley in the *Preiser Report* in 2009 and selected by *Novus Vinum* as one of the Top Ten Wines for Thanksgiving in 2008.

Drew is also gaining a national reputation for leading the way in bringing the tradition of beaujolais-nouveau-inspired wines—and harvest parties—to the California wine country. The family has recently begun making a small production of "Napa nouveau" from gamay noir ($17), which they release with much fanfare and merrymaking during the traditional third week of November.

The best way to learn more about the history of gamay in the Napa

Valley—and about the other wines they make at Andrew Lane Wines—
is to make an appointment for one of their winemaker tours. My favorite
is the signature Cheval Blanc breakfast with Drew in St. Helena. There
are local English muffins and homemade hillside jam, and Drew will
walk you through a private tasting of the family's wines in this unique
take on the breakfast of champions (for more information contact: coun-
trylanetours@andrewlanewines.com).

# CULINARY INSTITUTE
## OF AMERICA

2555 Main Street ✦ St. Helena
St. Helena Highway (Highway 29)
just south of the Krug Road intersection
*Tel:* 707.967.2320 ✦ www.ciachef.edu/California

O NE OF AMERICA'S MOST PRESTIGIOUS CULINARY SCHOOLS, THE CULINARY INSTITUTE OF AMERICA—KNOWN TO AFICIO-nados simply as the CIA—is well-known as home to the *Wine Spectator* Greystone Restaurant, where you can watch some of the area's most talented young chefs whip up local delights

(Sunday to Thursday 11:30AM to 9PM, Friday and Saturday 11:30AM to 10PM).

Less well known—but worth a trip when you are in the wine country—are the one-hour public cooking demonstrations (around $15) and the wine discovery courses offered at the Rudd Center for Professional Wine Studies (around $85). The wine discovery courses are led by a professional sommelier and focus on introducing passionate enthusiasts to some of the finer points of wine appreciation. If you are ready to get serious about your wine tasting, this is starting at the top. The campus also offers a variety of cooking courses geared toward home chefs.

# COOK ST. HELENA

1310 Main Street ✦ St. Helena

Downtown St. Helena

*Tel:* 707.963.7088

Tuesday *to* Saturday 11:30AM *to* 10PM, Sunday 5PM *to* 10PM

**L**OCATED ALONG MAIN STREET IN DOWNTOWN ST. HELENA, COOK IS THE PLACE THE LOCAL WINEMAKERS CONSIDER their special joint. And it's easy to see why. The atmosphere here is busy and cheerful, and, on most nights if you want to try some of Jude Wilmoths's signature braised short ribs with scallion whipped potatoes, advance reservations are a must.

But afternoons are actually my favorite time to stop in for a glass of wine and a plate of homemade pasta at the bar, where I can admire the selection of wines on offer by small family vintners. The pasta dishes are authentic regional Italian delights, and, if you take your espresso to one of the small tables by the window, it's the perfect place to watch this part of the world go by. Most entrees are around $20.

The wine list emphasizes small family vineyards, and provides a great chance to try wines made by some of the valley's smallest producers, many of which aren't open even by appointment. If you didn't get a chance to visit the Frias Family Vineyards, you can sample their sauvignon blanc by the glass. Run by two generations of the Frias family—founders Manuel and Maria and two of their sons, Fernando and Manny—this small winery is part of the California renaissance of small producers; with only about fifteen acres planted to vine, the production today is still limited to around 3,500 cases a

year (415.566.2419, www.friasfamilyvineyard.com).

This is also the place to try a bottle of the Bressler Vineyards cabernet sauvignon, a super-premium and ultra-boutique vintage that sells out within a few months of bottling every year. Bob and Stacey Bressler—who left careers in high tech for a life in the wine country—make fewer than 500 cases a year from grapes grown just around the corner on a small family vineyard in St. Helena (www.bresslervineyards.com).

If you prefer to bring your own recent discovery, corkage is $10.

# CINDY'S
# BACKSTREET KITCHEN

1327 Railroad Avenue ✦ St. Helena
Downtown St. Helena, one block east of
Highway 29/Main Street
*Tel:* 707.963.1200 ✦ www.cindysbackstreetkitchen.com
Daily 11:30AM to 10PM, shorter hours during the winter

LOCATED ON ONE OF THE BACK STREETS THAT RUN ALONG THE EAST SIDE OF HIGHWAY 29 IN ST. HELENA, CINDY'S Backstreet Kitchen is a local favorite for fine dining. Walking down the courtyard path to the front door, you get the feeling you're stopping by a friend's home for dinner, and that's the whole idea here. The restaurant is a converted farmhouse, and the bar in the front room is a lively scene on most nights.

But if the atmosphere is welcoming, that doesn't mean the food isn't serious. Owned and operated by chef Cindy Pawleyn, who also runs several other acclaimed restaurants in the valley, the menu highlights local ingredients. There are slow-cooked main dishes from the wood-fired oven, excellent steak frites, and creative daily specials. The best time to come, however, is on Wednesday night when Cindy hosts a supper club. Each week it's a different *prix fixe* menu ($45) inspired by national cuisines from around the world. Corkage is $15, and the extensive wine list features many of the valley's small family wineries.

# NAPA VALLEY OLIVE MANUFACTURING COMPANY

835 Charter Oak Avenue ✦ St. Helena
St. Helena Highway (Highway 29) at
Charter Oak Drive, just south of St. Helena
*Tel.* 707.963.4173

I F YOU NEED FIXINGS FOR A BACK LANE PICNIC, LOCALS WILL SEND YOU TO THE NAPA VALLEY OLIVE MANUFACTURING Company, which sells some of the wine country's most coveted olive oils and a wide selection of cheeses, provisions, breads, and homemade charcuterie.

The Particelli and Lucchesi families have been doing business out of this roadside barn since the 1930s, and you can find their popular and quirky little shop just down the street from the celebrated Tra Vigne restaurant. Here, your bill is totted up on butcher paper, and the only register is a cash box crammed with crumpled ones and fives. Word on the street is that this place was the original inspiration for the celebrated Oakville Grocery further down the valley.

# THE WHITE BARN

2727 Sulphur Springs Avenue ✦ St. Helena
St. Helena Highway (Highway 29) to
Sulphur Springs Avenue, south of downtown St. Helena
*Tel:* 707.963.3408 ✦ www.thewhitebarn.org

HIS 1872 CIVIL WAR ERA CARRIAGE HOUSE TURNED PRIVATE THEATRE IS ONE OF THE TREASURES OF THE NAPA Valley and one taste of the close community ties that the locals nurture in this special corner of the world.

Founded in the 1980s by Nancy Garden, the White Barn epitomizes the North Bay ethos. It's a local playhouse and meeting space where actors, musicians, artists, and writers come to perform—with all proceeds going to support charitable causes both locally and internationally. There are poetry salons and French jazz performances, holiday theatricals and barn dances, as well music and drama representing a broad range of talent from the Bay Area and beyond.

Complimentary Napa wines are served during the intermissions, donated by vintners from across the region. Performances have benefited everything from the Calistoga community pool to economic opportunities for women in developing countries. But the White Barn isn't just about supporting good causes—it's also a charming and beautiful spot, where after a long day on the tasting trail visitors can enjoy some of the best after-hours entertainment in the area.

CHAPTER SEVEN

# ST. HELENA HIGHWAY

## WINERIES

## RESTAURANTS AND PICNIC PROVISIONS

## DIVERSIONS

The St. Helena Highway connects Napa and Calistoga and, running along the western side of the valley, is the region's main tasting route. Driving northward into the heart of Napa, you'll see billboard after billboard welcoming you to some of California's biggest and best-known wineries, places where tour buses and limousines roll in hourly and visitors can luxuriate in the splendor of vast gardens and gleaming tasting rooms. But, while the St. Helena Highway might not be exactly a back lane, along this familiar route there are dozens of small family wineries—off the highway and in the small towns of Yountville, Oakville, and Rutherford—that would be easy to miss.

The wine country grew up around these kinds of places—family farms and old vineyards. Some have quietly been making wonderful small-production wines for the better part of a century. Others are old ghost wineries that have been reinvigorated by people who have come to the wine country more recently. Hidden in plain sight, these are some of the gems of the valley.

# V MADRONE WINERY

3199 St. Helena Highway (Highway 29) ✦ St. Helena
St. Helena Highway (Highway 29) just north of Ehlers Lane
*Tel.* 707.963.3573 ✦ www.vmadrone.com
Tasting by appointment only

ALTHOUGH CHRIS AND PAULINE TILLEY ONLY OPENED THE TASTING ROOMS AT V MADRONE WINERY IN 2008—OPENING day was the seventy-fifth anniversary of the end of Prohibition—this place has a long and storied history in the valley. Set off on the west side of the St. Helena Highway, the rambling old Victorian home is the original site of the nineteenth-century Hersch family winery, established in 1880. That makes V Madrone one of the valley's celebrated ghost wineries, the county's evocative term for those earliest wineries founded before the eighteenth amendment ended commercial viniculture for more than a decade.

Many of those first wineries were torn down or left to fall to ruins, and the hills above the valley floor are dotted with their picturesque remains. With property along a main thoroughfare, however, those early owners of what is now V Madrone had other plans. They turned their winery into a lodge and restaurant—which did double duty on late nights during the 1930s as a jazz-age speakeasy where the wine still flowed.

This eight-acre estate also bears the traces of a far more ancient history. When Chris and Pauline set about restoring the historic barn on the property and refitting it as a barrel storage facility, archaeologists discovered that this plot of land, set creek-side amid towering stands of coastal redwood trees and live oaks, was once a major flaking facility where the

valley's Native Americans produced arrowheads. And be sure to ask to see the prehistoric petroglyph set in the stone just outside what is now the winery's front door.

Chris and Pauline bought the property on their honeymoon, and it's easy to see why anyone would fall in love with this spot. Today the couple runs a small winery on the land, where the focus is on making around 1,200 cases a year of well-crafted estate cabernet sauvignon, Carneros chardonnay, an old-vine zinfandel, and a petit-sirah-based blend. *Wine Enthusiast* awarded their first release—the 2004 cabernet sauvignon—93 points, and all indications point to great things in the vintages to come. Tasting here is intimate and friendly; visitors stroll the vineyards and can relax under the shade trees that feel miles from the tourist trail. Wines range from $45–$100, and the tasting fee is $25. If you happen to be in the valley over St. Patrick's Day, the winemakers celebrate their family heritage with legendary Irish enthusiasm.

# EHLERS ESTATE

3222 Ehlers Lane ✦ St. Helena
St. Helena Highway (Highway 29) & Ehlers Lane
*Tel.* 707.963.5972 ✦ www.ehlersestate.com
Tasting Tuesday & Saturday by appointment only

**S**ET JUST BACK FROM NAPA'S MAIN THOROUGHFARE, HIGHWAY 29, EHLERS ESTATE IS AN HISTORIC WINERY WITH one of the valley's most unique stories. Founded by Jean Leducq, a wine enthusiast who was also heir to a French laundry fortune, Ehlers Estate could have been just another ultra-premium, high-profile winery. And while it does fit that bill, the most amazing part of this family story is what Jean Leducq, who died from cardiac disease in 2002, did with that fortune. Today Ehlers Estate is the asset of a medical trust, which funds university research into heart disease to the tune of $30 million annually. If the French paradox discovered that wine is good for the heart, this is one winery helping to prove the point.

Ehlers also makes excellent wines, and, if you would like to add an educational component to your tasting experience in the Napa Valley, the winery offers some of the county's best programs. Visitors can register online for a visit that includes a tour of the organic vineyards and historic winery, followed by a sit-down tasting of their estate wines, which are paired with small plates. Ehlers has been making wines with a "green" approach since 2003.

If Ehlers is leading the way in sustainable viniculture in the wine country, this is also a place with deep historical roots in the valley. Vine-

yards were first planted on this property in the nineteenth century by Bernard Ehlers, who built the stone winery, another of Napa's ghost wineries, that is still used as part of the production facility. In the summer, the courtyard just beyond is shaded by an orchard of olive trees that have stood for more than a century, and the lush kitchen gardens are reminiscent of Jean Leducq's first foray into the winemaking business—when he purchased a vineyard in Virginia on land where Thomas Jefferson had once grown grapes and run a gentleman's farm.

The estate is comprised of thirty-nine acres planted to vine—mainly the Napa Valley's celebrated cabernet sauvignon, but Ehler also produces a merlot, cabernet franc, and one of the few St. Helena-appellated sauvignon blancs. The wines range from $25–100, with most in the $45 range, and the annual production is around 6,500 cases. Passionate cooks will also want to look for Ehlers's limited release estate cabernet sauvignon vinegar, made from the half-empty bottles left in the tasting room at the end of the day. Tasting fee $35.

# ALLORA VINEYARDS

3244 Ehlers Lane ✦ St. Helena
St. Helena Highway (Highway 29) & Ehlers Lane
*Tel.* 707.963.6071 ✦ www.alloravineyards.com
Tasting by appointment only

TASTING AT ALLORA VINEYARDS TAKES PLACE IN THE WINE CELLARS BUILT UNDERNEATH THE CHEERFUL YELLOW stucco home surrounded by olive trees and vineyards that Terry and Nancy Klein purchased in the 1990s. Terry grew up here in the heart of the Napa Valley and made his name working in architectural plastering, but making wine had always been on his mind.

The property had been recognized as ideal for growing grapes as early as the 1800s. The Kleins began growing grapes on the fifteen-acre property in the late 1990s, and the first vintage was only a hundred cases; now there are ten acres of organically farmed vineyards, planted to cabernet sauvignon, cabernet franc, and petite sirah, and during the harvest the grapes are hand-

picked and hand sorted

The winery, which takes its name from an Italian expression that roughly translates to "well, then," now produces around 1,200 cases of five different wines: a reserve cabernet sauvignon, a Bordeaux blend, a cabernet franc, a sangiovese and cabernet blend, and a petite sirah wine (prices from $40–100). Here, the emphasis isn't on maximizing yields but on making a wine the family can be proud of, so during the growing season they "drop" almost half the fruit on the cabernet vines—wine-maker's lingo for the process of pruning a proportion of unripe fruit early in the season to ensure richly concentrated flavors and sugars in the grapes that remain come fall. The wines are barrel-fermented and made with wild yeasts, and the minimal sulfides added to the wines are organic, so wine enthusiasts prone to headaches are less likely to suffer for their pleasures.

The winemaker's tour and tasting is hosted by candlelight in the underground wine library. You'll want to ask Terry about his unique imported crystal stemware collection, with glasses that are a modern adaptation of a traditional Italian design able to open the bouquet of a wine, and a stylish decanter that is easy to clean (prices starting at $40). After, you can stroll through the family's lush Tuscan-style gardens or take a peek at the vineyards just beyond. The fee for tasting is $20, waived with purchase.

# STONY HILL VINEYARD

3331 St. Helena Highway (Highway 29) ✦ St. Helena
Call for directions
*Tel:* 707.963.2636 ✦ www.stonyhillvineyard.com
Tasting Monday *to* Friday, by appointment only

**T**HE ROAD THAT LEADS UP TO STONY HILL VINEYARD IS A SINGLE-LANE TRACK JUST BEFORE THE ENTRANCE TO THE Bale Mill State Park, and here the moss hangs low from the oak and madrone trees before giving way at the crest of the hill to sweeping views of the Napa Valley. Among all the many charming wineries in the valley, Stony Hill is a standout. Wine tasting out in the summer tasting room—a patio table with the world at your feet—it is easy to find yourself entertaining thoughts of never going home.

Peter McCrea's father first bought this 160-acre property in the 1940s and, in the years after the Second World War, planted it to mostly chardonnay and German varietals using a tractor he bought secondhand from one of the local ranchers. He established Stony Hill Vineyard— bonded California winery no. 4461—in 1952, long before the winemaking renaissance that turned Napa Valley into a household name. In fact, this longevity makes Stony Hill one of the oldest wineries in the valley still owned by the same family. (The oldest is Krug, just down on the valley floor.)

Today, the estate winery is run by Peter and wife Willinda, and they make a unique style of wine that also happens to be one of the great bargains of the Napa Valley. The average production is around 5,000 cases

of wine a year, including a Chablis-style chardonnay ($36) made with no malolactic fermentation and in neutral oak barrels. "It's chardonnay that tastes like chardonnay," Peter will tell you. Winemaker Mike Chelini—who has been with Stony Hill for more than thirty years and is only the second winemaker in the estate's history—also makes delicious drier-style Riesling and Gewürztraminer wines ($20 range) and a handcrafted Semillon dessert wine made from grapes originally found at France's legendary Château d'Yquem ($15).

There is no cost for the tasting and tour, which includes a trip up to the winery, where Riesling is still made in fifty-year-old German barrels and where visitors can take a step back into California history to see what this valley must have been like in the beginning.

ELIZABETH SPENCER WINES

ELIZABETH SPENCER          0.0 mi

1.0 mi      HONIG

1.1 mi      ROUND POND

Niebaum-Coppola's
RUBICON ESTATE          0.3 mi

1.7 mi      FROG'S LEAP

2.7 mi   AUBERGE DU SOLEIL

2796 mi   CHARLOTTESVILLE

2860 mi    PHILADELPHIA

3084 mi    THE

# ELIZABETH SPENCER

1165 Rutherford Road ✦ Rutherford
St. Helena Highway (Highway 29) &
Highway 128 east/Rutherford Road
*Tel:* 707.963.6067 ✦ www.elizabethspencerwines.com
Tasting daily 10AM & 6PM, appointment
strongly suggested during summer

JUST A STONE'S THROW FROM THE ST. HELENA HIGHWAY AND TUCKED AWAY IN THE SMALL VILLAGE OF RUTHERFORD is one of the wine country's most charming finds. The tasting room at Elizabeth Spencer Wines—the shared passion of Elizabeth Pressler and Spencer Graham—is the original brick post office of the village.

Today, the 1872 building, covered in the summer months with a profusion of morning glory vines and jasmine, has been transformed into a retreat for the senses.

Elizabeth and Spencer met and married when she was launching her wine-marketing company in Napa and he was a chef and fine wine distribu-

⠀⠀ ⠀ the mid-Atlantic region. Creating their own wines and brand seemed like a perfect way to celebrate their partnership, so, in 1998, they produced their first vintages and subsequently opened the Rutherford tasting room in 2006. Now, visitors gather around the cozy zinc bar or, during the summer months, head out to the enclosed garden just beyond the patio door. Flagship wines are the cabernet sauvignon offerings, but fans of northern California sauvignon blanc, chardonnay, pinot noir, and syrah wines will also find something to delight. These are excellent small-lot wines, and, priced in the $40–75 range, they over-deliver for the money.

The signature tasting starts at $20, and appointments are recommended but not required, although devoted wine aficionados will want to plan ahead and reserve a spot at one of the two daily appellation experiences ($40; 10:45AM and 4PM), where four cabernets from different regions are poured, as well as a mystery wine, providing a chance to experience firsthand the influence of appellation on a wine. Groups can reserve private tastings in the garden or in the tasting cottage.

If you're looking for a special event during your visit, it's worth getting on the winery's email list (email: tastingroom@elizabethspencerwines.com). Elizabeth Spencer holds several annual events at its tasting room, including an oysters and sauvignon blanc pairing in the spring and a paella tasting with hearty red wine in the fall. Fans quaff the latest wine releases, paired with delicious food, at these convivial Napa occasions that are open to the public.

# LONG MEADOW RANCH

1796 St. Helena Highway (Highway 29) ✦ Rutherford
*Tel:* 707.963.4555 ✦ www.longmeadowranch.com
Open seasonally Wednesday *to* Friday 1PM *to* 6PM,
Saturday 9AM *to* 5PM, and by appointment during winter

**S**ET ON 650 ACRES OF RANCH LAND IN THE MAYACAMAS MOUNTAINS, LONG MEADOW IS A GOURMET DELIGHT IN THE Napa Valley, and, if you are looking for a Slow Food experience in the wine country, look no further. The property—run by Ted, Laddie, and Christopher Hall—boasts the oldest olive orchards in the county, which produce a high-quality boutique olive oil from the fruit of trees first planted in the 1870s. The family works closely with some of Napa's most celebrated restaurants to provide them with great ingredients, including organic vegetables from their extensive gardens, and meat from a herd of grass-fed cattle.

Of course, Long Meadow Ranch also produces some of the hillside wines that have made Napa famous. There's a rich mountain cabernet sauvignon, a proprietary cabernet-based blend, a sauvignon blanc, and a sangiovese (most $20–45), as well as one of the few handcrafted grappas made in the valley ($35).

Visitors can stop by to sample the wines and shop the farmers market for picnic fixings when the ranch is open, but it's the organized tasting tours that are unforgettable. On Saturday mornings at 10:30AM, the family offers an estate tour in a vintage Swiss Army Pinzgauer that includes an olive oil and wine tasting ($35). If you'd rather walk, they lead vineyard tour and tasting hikes that include a visit to the caves, a stroll through the olive orchard, a sampling of the different ranch products, and, of course, spectacular scenery ($50). The real extravaganza is the private estate picnic—which includes either a guided hike or a back-roads jeep tour—with a lunch of grass-fed beef, ranch-raised produce, and the Long Meadow Ranch wines ($150).

# MACAULEY VINEYARDS

P.O. Box 398 ✦ Rutherford

Tasting off site, call for details

*Tel.* 707.963.0263 ✦ www.macauleyvineyard.com

Tasting by appointment only

---

**M**ACAULEY VINEYARDS FIRST MADE ITS REPUTATION BACK IN THE 1980s AS A PREMIUM PRODUCER OF LATE-harvest sauvignon blanc wines, when the winery was founded by Ann Macauley Watson, one of the first women to graduate from Harvard with an M.B.A. and, back then, one of the few women in the wine business as well. She bought nine

acres of vineyard property just south of the Old Bale Mill on the St. Helena Highway and planned a life in the wine country.

Her son Mac, an avid wine collector, whose passion for fine vintages was ignited by a bottle of Château Lafite Rothschild that he shared with his dad as a teenager, revived the family label in 2001. From the start, the Macauley wines have received striking accolades. Mac's 2004 cabernet sauvignon, made by winemaker Kirk Venge, with fruit sourced from the legendary Beckstoffer To Kalon vineyard, was rated 96 points in *Wine Spectator*; the 2005 To Kalon earned 91 points in the *Wine Advocate* and Robert Parker's simple recommendation that "these wines merit attention." There is also a small production of peppery zinfandel (wines from $35–150).

There are limited tasting appointments available ($45, credited toward purchase). The private winemaker's tour starts out at the kitchen table of Mac's vineyard ranch home. The total production is 800 cases annually.

# CHANTICLEER WINES

4 Vineyard View Drive ✦ Yountville
Call for directions
*Tel.* 707.945.0566 ✦ www.chanticleerwine.com
Tasting by appointment only

WHEN GEORGE AND CADDY GRODAHL CAME TO THE NAPA VALLEY IN THE MID-1990s AND BOUGHT THIS forty-acre hillside property, they named their vineyards Morningside after their former home in Kent, England, where they could see the storied Pilgrim's Way trail that led to Canterbury just at the bottom of the drive. Their vision was to sell the grapes to the big wineries, perhaps making a few cases of homemade wines out in the garage for their family and friends, and enjoy life at a slower pace.

The trouble was that those bottles were good, and in 2000, working with winemaker Chris Deardon, the family released their first vintage at Chanticleer, taking the name of the winery from the quick-witted rooster in Chaucer's *Canterbury Tales.* Today, they produce around 1,000 cases of premium super-Tuscan-style wines, one a signature Napa cabernet sauvignon ($58) and the other principally sangiovese ($45)—a grape that is suddenly getting a lot more attention here in the valley and is the essential component of Italian wines made in the Chianti region. It can be a tricky grape to grow, but it's gaining popularity for its rich flavors.

With such a small production, George likes to joke that Chanticleer is a stealth winery, and most of his visitors do learn about his wines through word-of-mouth. And what's not to be enthusiastic about? The

tasting room is a charming candlelit wine cellar dug into the hillside just beyond the family's home, where George will pour the wines and lead you through a tasting that includes a gourmet cheese selection and locally made chocolates from Napa's Le Belge Chocolatier (www.lebel-gechocolatier.com). After, there's time to take in the views of Stag's Leap and the valley floor and to luxuriate in one of Napa's most intimate tours. There is no charge for tasting.

# KEEVER VINEYARDS

26 Vineyard View Drive ✦ Yountville

Call for directions

*Tel.* 707.944.0910 ✦ www.keevervineyards.com

Tasting by appointment only

**J**UST OVER THE CREST OF A HILL ON A SMALL ROAD IN THE WESTERN FOOTHILLS OF THE NAPA VALLEY, JUST DOWN the road from Chanticleer, is the Tuscan-style winery at Keever Vineyards, one of the area's newcomers. Run by the husband-and-wife team of Bill and Olga Keever, along with their son Jason, this two-generation family estate—a "retirement plan gone beautifully wrong"—only opened to the public in 2006.

Bill graduated from Napa High School in 1963. His family had made its home in the valley for the better part of a decade, but Bill spent his working life in other parts of the state, later living abroad with Olga and their two children. He jokes that, when he and his wife retired to this twenty-one-acre vineyard property, the plan was to sell some grapes and spend their days playing golf. But hillside cabernet sauvignon is a prized commodity in the wine country, and their vineyard manager encouraged them to make some of their own wines.

Working with winemaker Celia Welch—*Food &*

*Wine* magazine's winemaker of the year for 2008—today Keever makes a small range of wines annually, including a signature estate 100% cabernet sauvignon ($90), made with fruit that has never left the property. The winery also produces a 50-50 Bordeaux-style blend of cabernet and merlot, some syrah, and a great fruity sauvignon blanc (all in the $28–50 range).

The spacious tasting room has views out over the eastern hills of the valley, as far as Mount George and Atlas Peak, and there are deep leather armchairs where you can catch your breath if all that wine tasting is proving too exhausting. The tasting ($20) includes a tour of the family's vineyards, the state-of-the-art gravity-flow winery, and the hillside caves, which by some wonder of acoustics have a special whisper spot, which might just be the wine country's most unique spot for a wedding proposal.

# RUDD WINERY
# AND VINEYARDS

500 Oakville Cross Road ✦ Oakville

Silverado Trail *at* Oakville Cross Road

*Tel:* 707.944.8577 ✦ www.ruddwines.com

Tasting by appointment only

I N THE WINEMAKING WORLD, THIS CORNER OF OAKVILLE IS KNOWN AS THE TENDERLOIN OF NAPA, AND THE FIFTY-FIVE-acre estate vineyards that are home to the Rudd Winery produce some of the most highly lauded boutique production wines in the valley. The winery is owned by Leslie Rudd and his wife Susie; Rudd is a name that many dedicated gourmets will recognize. Leslie made his fortune in the world of business, first as a wine and spirits distributor and later as the founder of Dean & DeLuca.

Rudd might not be struggling for capital, but it's still a small family winery that produces fewer than 10,000 cases a year, mainly a range of Napa Valley cabernet sauvignon and Bordeaux-blend wines (most from $65–125). Because Susie is a particular fan of sauvignon blanc, there is an estate wine from the family's Mount Veeder vineyards ($45), as well as a Sonoma County chardonnay ($65) made from the same vines that produced the fruit in the 1973 Château Montelena chardonnay—the wine that won the 1976 Judgment of Paris for the Californians.

The $50 tasting fee at Rudd Winery includes a winemaker's tour of the production facilities and the estate gardens, and a chance to sample a range of the family's ultra-premium wines.

There is also a small family second label on the other side of the valley, the Edge Hill Vineyard Company (500 Oakville Cross Road), located on an historic property that the family began restoring in the late 1990s. The site of a famous pre-Prohibition winery, these vineyards produced the most expensive wines made in California during the last decades of the nineteenth century and, later, the property was the home of one of the state's earliest award-winning distilleries. The total case production at Edge Hill today is around a hundred cases a year, and the five acres of estate vineyards are mostly planted to southern Rhône field blends such as mourvèdre, grenache, carignan, and alicante bouché (wines around $100).

# BISTRO JEANTY

6510 Washington Street ✦ Yountville
Exit St. Helena Highway (Highway 29) at Yountville,
east on California Drive to Washington Street
Tel. 707.944.0103 ✦ www.bistrojeanty.com
Monday to Sunday 11:30AM to 10:30PM

THE FRENCH KNOW HOW TO DO BISTRO DINING LIKE NO ONE ELSE—UNDERSTATED ELEGANCE AND EXCELLENT FOOD served up with a sense of community spirit and a warm welcome—and if I were to choose a favorite spot in the Napa Valley to settle in for a long lunch or a romantic dinner in the Parisian style, it would be Bistro Jeanty. The owner and chef Philippe Jeanty hails from the Champagne region of France and first came to the wine country in the 1970s as part of the team sent over to open the signature restaurant at Domaine Chandon. He opened the doors to his own bistro in 1998, and it was immediately recognized as one of the best new restaurants in the Bay area.

Set just along the main street in the picturesque little town of Yountville, where you can while away an afternoon in the local antique shops and the nearby shopping gallery, Bistro Jeanty can be recognized by the brightly colored flowers pouring out of the window boxes and the candy-stripe red-and-white awning that sets the cheerful and intimate tone. Signature dishes include escargots served with pastis butter, home-smoked trout salad, a fabulous coq au vin, and, for those who like their beef blue, steak tartare with frites. Most entrees are priced at $20–25, and corkage is a reasonable $15.

# REDD

6480 Washington Street ✦ Yountville
Exit St. Helena Highway at California Drive,
north on Washington Street
*Tel:* 707.944.2222 ✦ www.reddnapavalley.com
Daily 11:30AM *to* 2:30PM, 5:30PM *to* 9:30PM

A HIGH-END LOCAL FAVORITE, CHEF RICHARD REDDINGTON'S WINE COUNTRY RESTAURANT IS AN OASIS OF CONTEMporary modernist décor. If you're looking for an elegant evening out and willing to splurge a bit on some formally presented cuisine, this is where the valley's winemakers and entrepreneurs come for great food in the new California style. The food is consistently excellent. Entrees run around $30, and, at $25, the corkage fee is on the expensive side. But there is an expansive local wine list, and this is a place where you can try wines you won't find anywhere else.

Among those undiscovered gems on the wine list, one of my favorites is the wine from Parry Cellars (www.parrycellars.com). Sue and Stephen Parry own a little postage stamp of a vineyard just off the Silverado Trail—so small that Stephen mows the cover crop himself each spring with his lawnmower. But it's a great *terroir* (the vineyard was first planted by David Abreu, of Screaming Eagle fame), where about 200 cases a year are produced of just one wine—a 100% estate, 100% cabernet sauvignon (around $100 on the wine list and $60 direct from the winery) that *Wine Enthusiast* has scored in the 90s. If you end up falling in love with the Parry cabernet sauvignon, you can buy it directly from the winery, but there is no tasting room.

# BALE GRIST MILL
# STATE HISTORIC PARK /
# BOTHE NAPA VALLEY STATE PARK

3369 St. Helena Highway (Highway 29)

St. Helena Highway (Highway 29)

just south of the Ehlers Lane intersection

*Tel.* 707.939.6188 ✦ www.parks.ca.gov/default.asp?page_id=482

Closed major holidays; overnight camping requires a permit

**D**URING THE LATTER PART OF THE NINETEENTH CENTURY, NAPA VALLEY FARMERS DIDN'T RELY ON THE PRODUCTION of grapes. In those pioneer days, wheat drove the local economy. So when Edward Turner Bale—a physician working for General Vallejo—settled down to make a home for himself in St. Helena in 1846, he built the water-powered gristmill that quickly became the center of public life in the valley.

The Bale mill continued to operate until the early decades of the twentieth century, and it has since been converted to a state historical park where visitors can tour the mill. On weekends, there are often milling demonstrations, where you can purchase bags of freshly ground cornmeal polenta. Nearby is the site of Napa's first church and the original nineteenth-century community cemetery.

Adjacent to the Bale Grist Mill State Historic Park is the 2,000-odd-acre Bothe Napa Valley State Park (pronounced *bow-thay*), which offers camping, swimming, and horseback riding, as well as a variety of hiking trails where you can stroll through redwood groves, visit the Native American garden, or dip your toes in the creek. The swimming pool is open from Memorial Day to Labor Day, and horseback riding tours are offered in the park by the Triple Creek Horse Outfit from April to October (707.887.8700, www.triplecreekhorseoutfit.com).

There is no charge to enter the Bale Historic Park but a small fee for the mill tours; the Bothe Napa State Park charges the standard California day-use fee (currently $6). There is an additional charge for use of the swimming pool. The grist mill is in operation when you see the "Milling Today" sign at the park entrance.

# NAPA VALLEY BALLOONS

6795 Washington Street ✦ Yountville
St. Helena Highway (Highway 29),
east on Yountville Cross Road *&* Washington Street
Morning launches from 4175 Solano Avenue ✦ Napa
*Tel:* 707.944.0228 ✦ www.napavalleyballoons.com

I F YOU THINK THE MOUNTAIN VIEWS FROM YOUR FAVORITE BACK LANE WINERY ARE SPECTACULAR, IMAGINE WHAT IT'S like flying over the Napa Valley at dawn in a hot air balloon. After landing, there's a field-side champagne breakfast. It's one of the quintessential wine-country experiences.

There are several professional balloon companies in the county, but one of the oldest and most renowned is Napa Valley Balloons, which is consistently voted the best balloon ride in the county. Balloons can accommodate up to ten people, and rates per person start at around $240 (winter and internet discounts often available). Reservations need to be made at least twenty-four hours in advance, and during the summer several weeks in advance is recommended. Balloons lift off at sunrise, and flight time is one hour.

# NAPA VALLEY BIKE TOURS

6795 Washington Street ✦ Building B ✦ Yountville
St. Helena Highway (Highway 29) & Madison Avenue,
at Washington Avenue intersection
*Tel.* 800.707.2453 ✦ www.napavalleybiketours.com

**T**HE IDEA OF CYCLING IN THE WARM CALIFORNIA SUNSHINE PAST THE VINEYARDS WHEN THE MUSTARD FIELDS ARE IN bloom is decidedly romantic. But if you are planning to spend your days tasting wines without the aid of dump buckets, it's also decidedly practical. Along the back lanes, coasting from one winery to the next, it's never a bad idea to gather one's wits with a small roadside picnic or perhaps even the briefest of naps.

Or, of course, you can make a serious endeavor of all this biking as well, if you like. The country roads in the wine country are among the world's most beautiful.

Whatever your pleasure, whether it's a bike tour or just an afternoon rental you're after, one of the friendliest spots to find two wheels is the Napa Valley Bike Tour company. The staff will happily advise you on some of the area's most scenic routes, and full-day rentals start at just $30. If you rent for a minimum of two days, bikes can be dropped off for you, then picked up, at any nearby hotels. With a bit of advance planning, wine-country connoisseurs can map out a series of unique tasting appointments; then, have your purchases either mailed directly from the winery or by a wine-shipping service, which will collect them from the vineyards and mail your new collection to you.

If advance planning is not your thing, you can leave it to the folks at Napa Valley Bike. They offer guided tours (either as part of a group or with a private guide; starting at around $115) that include a picnic lunch, pick-up and delivery of your wines, and help scheduling tasting appointments.

# CHAPTER EIGHT

# EASTERN VALLEYS
## INCLUDING
## CHILES VALLEY AND POPE VALLEY

**W**hile Howell Mountain was the first recognized sub-appellation in the Napa Valley and remains the most widely known eastern hillside AVA in the wine country, there are several wonderful small wineries tucked away in the mountains rising above the valley floor. Some of these wineries are located in distinct sub-appellations like the Chiles Valley AVA or the Pope Valley AVA, where unique microclimates and growing conditions help to create wines with a very particular character and expression of *terroir*. Other areas in these sometimes remote and wild valleys are simply part of the prestigious Napa Valley AVA, although areas like Pritchard Hill are well known to devoted wine aficionados.

The drive up to these wineries takes you along country roads, often through miles of undeveloped valley terrain, and you won't find any of those charming bistros back here. There aren't many gasoline stations either. But if what you are looking for is an experience of the landscape at its most beautifully bucolic and a chance to sample some wines that are unlike what you'll find down on the valley floor, these eastern hillside vineyards offer new discoveries.

# NICHELINI WINERY

2950 Sage Canyon Road ✦ St. Helena

Silverado Trail & Sage Canyon Road (Highway 128)

Tel 707.963.0717 ✦ www.nicheliniwinery.com

Tasting Saturday and Sunday 10AM & 5PM,

weekdays by appointment, closed holidays

THE NICHELINI FAMILY HAS BEEN MAKING WINES HERE IN THE EASTERN HILLS OF NAPA COUNTY SINCE THE 1890s, and their vintage farmhouse and tasting room might just be one of the most charming rustic little places you'll encounter out here as you head into the Chiles Valley. The family will tell you that they are the oldest continually operating winery in the Napa Valley, and a visit to them is a chance to step back into history and to get a glimpse of what the wine country must have been like just a couple of generations ago.

Nichelini specializes in making wines from fruit grown on family property in the Chiles Valley, including a chardonnay and a delicious sauvignon vert—made from the white Bordeaux muscadelle grape. There are also several red wines, ranging from the classic cabernet sauvignon and merlot varietals to a port-style dessert wine and a primitivo that recently took home a medal in the San Francisco International Wine Competition. Most wines around $30, and there is no charge for tasting.

# VOLKER EISELE FAMILY ESTATE

3080 Lower Chiles Valley Road ✦ St. Helena

Silverado Trail *to* Sage Canyon Road (Highway 128), east *to*
Chiles/Pope Valley Road, north *to* Lower Chiles Valley Road;
proceed half a mile *to* the winery

*Tel:* 707.965.9485 ✦ www.volkereiselefamilyestate.com

Tasting by appointment only

A GOOD WAY OUT OF TOWN ON A SMALL WINDING BACK LANE, YOU'LL COME ACROSS THE OLD WOODEN WINERY THAT IS home to the Volker Eisele Family Estate. The building was built in the 1870s, and with its weathered tin roof and bleached exterior there is something essentially Northern Californian about it all. Old fir floor planks creak pleasantly, and, on a hot summer day in the Napa Valley—because days can get hot in the

ine country, it's worth remembering that things stay a bit cooler up here at 1,200 feet.

Chiles Valley, an arm of the Napa Valley, is long and narrow, running from northwest to southeast, and the small family wineries in this region are making some of Napa County's most interesting new wines. But, even if Chiles Valley is just gaining widespread recognition as one of Napa's premium appellations, people have been quietly making excellent cabernet wines out here for generations. Volker and Liesel Eisele have been growing grapes in their fifty-acre vineyard since the mid-1970s, and today, along with their son Alexander, they release a small production of organic estate wines, mostly Bordeaux varietals, along with some semillon and sauvignon blanc. Replanting has all been on the original footprint of the l870s vineyard.

Volker and Liesel met while studying at the University of California, both having come to the Bay area from Germany. Curiously enough, few people know that there is a long tradition of German immigrants shaping winemaking in the Napa Valley despite the fact that at the end of the nineteenth and beginning of the twentieth century, they were a major presence in the wine country.

The Eisele family started out as growers and didn't release their first commercial vintage until the early 1990s. They now produce four different wines: Gemini, a crisp, white blend of sauvignon blanc and semillon that *Wine Enthusiast* recently gave 93 points and called "one of the best wines of its type" (2006 vintage); a beautifully complex cabernet sauvignon; their signature co-fermented Terzetto blend, made with cabernet sauvignon, cabernet franc, and merlot (ranging from $25–75); and a special reserve Alexander cabernet sauvignon—a minute production of just six barrels—sold only from the tasting room and in boxes of three ($375). The fee for tasting is $25.

# RUSTRIDGE BED AND BREAKFAST AND WINERY

2910 Lower Chiles Valley Road ✦ St. Helena

Silverado Trail *to* Sage Canyon Road (Highway 128), east *to* Chiles/Pope Valley Road, north *to* Lower Chiles Valley Road

*Tel.* 707.965.9353 ✦ www.rustridge.com

Tasting by appointment only

I F YOU ARE LONGING TO GET AWAY FOR A WINE COUNTRY WEEKEND BUT THE FANCY SPAS UP IN CALISTOGA AREN'T YOUR cup of tea, the RustRidge Winery—which does double duty as a bed and breakfast and as a working ranch and horse farm—is the kind of place where you can fall off the grid for a few days of real peace and quiet. During harvest, guests can watch the crush firsthand, and that's the kind of education in the life of a winemaker you won't find many places. If you visit during the other eleven months of the year, there are gourmet breakfasts, hiking trails, tennis courts, and even an on-site sauna to enjoy.

When you're not out wine tasting, of course. And wine tasting at RustRidge can begin right after a hearty breakfast. It's a great opportunity to discover the Chiles Valley, one of Napa's less familiar but most distinctive appellations. The valley is known for its production of claret-style zinfandel wines; RustRidge is also known for its chardonnay. The grape develops beautifully here at this elevation, where the nights can get cold even in the summer months.

The husband-and-wife team of Susan Meyer and Jim Fresquez run the ranch, which Susan's parents bought in the 1970s. Her father and

brothers planted the first vineyards on the property in 1975. Now Jim and Susan, with partner Kent Rosenblum, make seven different wines: the signature zinfandel and chardonnay wines; the highly acclaimed red and white blends, simply called (in a nod to the more than fifteen horses they keep in the stables) Racehorse Red and Racehorse White; a sauvignon blanc; a cabernet sauvignon; and a new release, petite sirah. The chardonnay and Racehorse Red have taken gold medals in the *San Francisco Chronicle* wine competition in recent years. There are plans to plant some pinot noir and petite sirah in the vineyards in the future; the climate should be ideal. Total case production is around 3,000, and the well-priced wines range from $22–40. Tasting is $15, waived with purchase; room rates, if you are hoping to take in the full RustRidge experience, are in the $165–350 range.

# PORTER FAMILY VINEYARDS

1189 Green Valley Road ✦ Napa
Silverado Trail *to* Coombsville Road
until Green Valley Road intersection
*Tel:* 707.265.7980 ✦ www.porterfamilyvineyards.com
Tasting by appointment only

A COUPLE OF MILLION YEARS OR SO AGO, COOMBSVILLE—THAT HILLSIDE CAULDRON DUG OUT OF THE NAPA VALLEY in the area between Mount George and Stag's Leap—was seashore property. Today, it rises five hundred feet above sea level and is increasingly renowned for its excellent production of cabernet sauvignon wines.

When Tom and Bev Porter left Silicon Valley to purchase their twenty-acre hillside vineyard property back in 2005, they set about excavating an underground cellar and production facility, and in the process discovered the fossilized footprints of ancient shorebirds. An image of those prehistoric sandpiper tracks appears on the labels of the Porter Family Vineyard wines, including their flagship cabernet sauvignon and robust syrah (in the $50–95 range). The family also releases a limited production of rosé wine and a proprietary blend (from $20–40) for a total estate wine production of just over 2,000 cases.

Now a two-generation family business, son Tim, daughter Heather, and son-in-law Steven are active in building and running the winery, and, as chance would have it, all the Porters have a scientific bent. Among them there are two electrical engineers, a computer scientist with a financial background, and a biologist—this means that vineyard manage-

ment on the property is high-tech. These steep hillside vineyards exhibit a variety of microclimates on the estate, which has been divided into thirty micro-blocks, each with different soil depths and water needs taken care of by a state-of-the-art wireless irrigation system, a vineyard sensory mesh network, and weather stations. There are thoughts of giving each plant in the vineyard its own radio-controlled identification tag. This is where science meets winemaking at its most ingenious.

But technology doesn't get in the way of the down-to-earth business of growing grapes up here in the mountain valleys above Napa. A visit to the Porter family winery includes a family-hosted tour of the vineyards and the caves, barrel tasting, and a behind-the-scenes introduction to how a great wine is produced. There's also a chance to sample some wines, of course. The charge for the two-hour tour is $50.

# AMIZETTA VINEYARDS

1099 Greenfield Road ✦ St. Helena

Silverado Trail *to* Howell Mountain Road/Conn Valley Road,
north on Greenfield Road

*Tel:* 707.963.1460 ✦ www.amizetta.com

Tasting by appointment only

---

T UCKED FAR UP INTO THE HILLS TO THE EAST OF THE VALLEY FLOOR, AMIZETTA IS WELL OFF THE BEATEN PATH. But it would be a shame to miss either the beauty of this pastoral retreat or this special little winery run by the husband-and-wife team of Spencer and Amizetta Clark— the latter a fifteenth-generation direct descendant of Pocahontas.

Back in the 1970s, when they purchased the property, Napa wasn't yet known for its hillside vineyards. They planted the land to grapes themselves in the early 1980s, intending to sell the fruit to some of the high-end wineries cropping up in the valley. Before long, of course, they were producing their own wines, and released their first cabernet sauvignon in 1985. Today the winery produces around 3,500 cases a year, focusing on cabernet sauvignon and red Bordeaux varietals, including a cabernet,

merlot, and cabernet franc blend called Complexity, and a lighthearted blend called Rock'n Red, a tribute to Spencer's second career as musician and songwriter.

Tasting takes place amid the sweet smells of oak barrels at an old pine table in the cave, where the year-round temperature is an ideal sixty-three degrees and where the soothing sounds of a bubbling spring weren't part of any grand plan—they discovered it when excavating. Beyond the door are beautiful gardens and spectacular views of their hillside vineyards overlooking Lake Hennessey and the Napa Valley. Tours are by appointment only, and there is no charge for tasting. The wines run from $25–100.

# CHAPPELLET

1581 Sage Canyon Road ✦ St. Helena
Silverado Trail *to* Highway 128/Sage Canyon Road heading east
*Tel:* 707.963.7136 ✦ www.chappellet.com
Tasting by appointment only

**U**P IN THE FOOTHILLS ALONG THE EASTERN RANGE OF NAPA, VISITORS TO THE WINE COUNTRY WILL FIND SOME of the most picturesque back lanes in the county. Here, winding country roads lead past overgrown madrone forests, and there are distant views of mountain valleys that seem to promise new discoveries around every turn.

One of those discoveries should be Chappellet. Unless, of course, you've already heard of its wines—this was one of the first cult wineries in Napa. Although Robert Parker called the 1969 cabernet sauvignon one of the greatest American wines ever made, Chappellet has never rested on its laurels—it continues to make on the order of 30,000 cases a year of some of Napa's most acclaimed wines.

The winery was founded back in the 1960s as a family affair, and it is still run by Donn Chappellet and his wife Molly. Three of their six children today are actively involved in the daily operation of the business, and the winery still retains a down-to-earth approach to making wine. Visitors walk past Donn's modest desk in the front room on the way to a tasting, and the place feels like old California. Lemon trees and flowering cacti are set against wooden barns, and the V.I.P. vineyard tour (a few times a week, by appointment, $75) is conducted from an old Pinzgauer Swiss Army jeep, where the rifle holders do double duty

as wine-glass keepers. From the mountainside tasting and picnic site on Pritchard Hill, there are breathtaking views of the vineyards, planted in terraces eerily reminiscent of an ancient Greek amphitheatre, and, in the far distance, Lake Hennessey and the mountains beyond.

The regular tasting and tour—$25 per person—is an equally intimate experience. Visitors sample Chappellet's organically farmed wines, including a small-lot chenin blanc and a range of red wines made from five Bordeaux varietals in the mountaintop production facility. Up here, where the hillside microclimate means cooler days and warmer nights, the wines are complex, subtle, and famously delicious, and, when the valley floor is seeming crowded and stuffy at the height of the tourist season, it's good to remember that there are places where you won't have to jostle for a spot at the bar.

# KULETO ESTATE

2470 Sage Canyon Road ✦ St. Helena
Silverado Trail ⁄ Highway 128/Sage Canyon Road heading east
Tel. 707.302.2209 ✦ www.kuletoestate.com
Tasting Monday ⁄ Saturday by appointment only

WATCHING THE SUNSET FROM THE ADIRONDACK CHAIRS UP AT KULETO ESTATE—PERCHED MORE THAN A thousand feet above the valley floor—is a little bit of bucolic bliss. In fact, this 761-acre estate, which restaurant designer Pat Kuleto calls home, feels refreshingly remote from the hustle and bustle of the loop—Napa's famous tasting circuit that takes millions of visitors a year up the St. Helena Highway and back down the Silverado Trail.

The entrance to Kuleto is a big gate off a country road, and from there it's still a slow, stately drive up the hillside. At the top, you'll find the tasting room in the welcoming Tuscan-style lodge, where everything is rough-hewn wood and warm stone. After sampling some wines at the bar, you can tour the property, which includes eighty-five acres of estate vineyards as well as lush, fanciful gardens, olive groves, and a paddock where the ranch livestock is raised. At the end of the tour, you'll have time to sample more wine and settle in on your own and enjoy the views.

Kuleto offers two tasting options: a wine-and-cheese pairing that includes an extensive estate tour ($35) or the option to add to that tasting a luxurious food and wine extravaganza that features hors d'oeuvres of seasonal ranch-raised gourmet delicacies ($95). If you are planning to visit in the summer, as I did at the boat tours of the private lake; they are offered occasionally.

The annual production at Kuleto is around 8,000 cases of estate wine, and, unsurprisingly given the hillside location of these Napa vineyards, the emphasis is on cabernet sauvignon wines, which regularly earn points in the 90s from *Wine Spectator*. Kuleto also produces chardonnay, rosé, pinot noir, and a stellar sangiovese; wines range from $20–125, with most in the $60 range.

# HEIBEL RANCH VINEYARDS

1241 Adams Street ✦ Suite 1043 ✦ St. Helena
Tasting off site, call or email for directions
*Tel.* 707.968.9289 ✦ www.hrvwines.com
Tours by appointment only

WINE TASTING AT HEIBEL RANCH VINEYARDS WITH PROPRIETOR TRENT GHIRINGHELLI IS SAFARI STYLE, and the only tasting room is the tailgate of a vintage baby blue U.S. Navy Jeep up on a mountaintop with long views of the Pope Valley. Sitting here above the fog line, sipping some wine, and taking it all in is what the back lane experience is all about.

Visitors to these ranch vineyards—owned and operated by Trent, his mother Helen, and stepfather Bruce Nelson—travel more than a mile off the county road, through ancient stands of redwood trees and along ridges with gnarled manzanita, as part of the winemaker's tour. This 186-acre hillside property is the parcel of land the family retained when they sold the Aetna Springs Resort, long a favorite haunt of old Hollywood and a piece of California history. Here, Ronald Reagan announced his first run for the governorship in the 1960s.

Heibel Ranch—the name is a nod to Helen's father, George Bennett Heibel, who purchased Aetna Springs Resort back in 1945—released its first vintage in 2006, and the wine sold out in a matter of months. The estate still makes just one wine, fewer than 200 cases a year of a proprietary Napa Valley red blend called Lappa's ($32), made with cabernet sauvignon, zinfandel, and a bit of petite sirah. It's grown on their two-acre, certified organic, estate vineyard that the family cleared on weekends and farms by hand. As the vineyards develop, there are plans to add a single-vineyard-designate cabernet sauvignon. The tasting fee is $25.

# CHAPTER NINE

# LOS CARNEROS
## AND ENVIRONS
# SOUTH OF NAPA

With one foot in Sonoma County and the other foot in Napa, the southern AVA known as Los Carneros—named after the nearby Carneros Creek and meaning simply "the ram" in Spanish—is cooled on hot summer days by the fog that rolls in from San Pablo Bay. The result is a cool-climate *terroir* at the southern tip of the wine country, an area famous for its pinot noir, chardonnay, and sparkling wines. With easy access to both downtown Napa and the historic plaza in the city of Sonoma, there are plenty of options to combine sightseeing and good food with tasting at some of the region's most accessible and interesting small wineries.

# BOURASSA VINEYARDS

190 Camino Oruga ✦ Napa
Napa/Vallejo Highway (Highway 29/12) south of Napa between
North Kelly Road and Jameson Canyon Road (Highway 12)
*Tel.* 707.254.4922 ✦ www.bourassavineyards.com
Tasting by appointment only

THE TASTING ROOM AT BOURASSA VINEYARDS IS IN A COMMERCIAL PARK OFF HIGHWAY 29, SOUTH OF THE CITY of Napa, and it might not fit the image of the rustic wine country that first comes to mind. But this is small-production winemaking at its most authentic, and it would be a mistake to miss a visit to what might just be one of the most intimate and inviting tasting rooms in the valley. Here, visitors sip wine in a candlelit tasting room, amid silver dump buckets and gleaming candelabra, and the feeling is surprisingly opulent and old-world. At Bourassa, the watchword is celebration, and it shows.

This small winery is the second-life dream of Vic Bourassa, who grew up in a French-Canadian family in New England and made his first career in real estate in Southern California. In the 1990s, he came to Napa, and from there it's the familiar story: he fell in love with the life-style and with the modest idea of making a little bit of wine. He started out working in some Napa Valley tasting rooms, took a few classes, and eventually went on to become the president of the Napa Valley Home Winemakers Association.

One afternoon, talking with his friend, the legendary winemaker Robert Mondavi, he brought out some of his homemade pinot noir,

and a delighted Mondavi polished off the bottle. But, despite making an excellent wine, Vic worried that it was too late to start a second career at fifty. He tells the story of how Mondavi reminded him that he didn't get his start in wine until he was fifty-five, and that turned out pretty well in the end. So in 2001, Vic released his first vintage—400 cases of wine.

Today, thanks to the strong reputation of his wines, Bourassa Vineyards produces around 5,000 cases. The winery is best known for its Bordeaux blends and for working with some unusual varietals, including petit verdot, although visitors will find everything from a crisp sauvignon blanc to a port-style dessert wine on offer.

Tasting is $15 and includes some of the essentials of wine education, tailored to your level of experience. This is a place where beginners can learn about the importance of oak in winemaking or how to distinguish

different varietals; more experienced or adventurous aficionados might want to reserve one of the blending seminars ($30), where you'll construct your own Bordeaux blend in a glass. Set aside some extra time if you want to take a morning tour that includes a visit to the Seguin Moreau cooperage just down the lane ($25), a fascinating, firsthand education in the traditional art of making barrels.

If you can't make it to Bourassa Vineyards on this trip, here's something else to consider: a winemaker's tasting party in your home. Vic travels widely and loves to share his passion for great wines.

# CEJA VINEYARDS

1016 Las Amigas Road ✦ Napa
Carneros/Sonoma Highway (Highway 12/121) to
Cuttings Wharf Road, keeping west on Las Amigas Road
*Tel.* 707.255.3954 ✦ www.cejavineyards.com
Tasting by appointment only

THE CEJA (PRONOUNCED SAY-HA) FAMILY CAME TO NAPA FROM MEXICO TO WORK IN THE VINEYARDS IN 1967, AND IT was nearly twenty years before they purchased their own land in the wine country. Today, the family—brothers Armando and Pedro, their wives Martha and Amelia, and several of their children—operate one of California's first modern wineries to be established by Mexican immigrants.

The four co-owners have more than a hundred years of winegrowing experience among them; all grew up working in the vineyards. Pedro and Amelia met there as teenagers. These days, Ceja Vineyards is a flourishing enterprise, with an estate tasting room out along the back lanes of the Carneros AVA and a downtown tasting salon and art gallery. Tasting in the Carneros takes place in the cozy vintage ranch house, where you can enjoy sampling the wines with the vineyards just beyond the glass doors. At the Napa tasting salon (see page 34), you can sample Ceja wines—or come for the Saturday evening salsa dancing (no cover, and free lessons beforehand).

The family makes ten different wines, ranging from Carneros chardonnay and pinot noir wines to a Napa Valley cabernet sauvignon, and a botrytis white port-style dessert wine of chardonnay and sauvignon blanc, and a syrah port. A range of cooler-climate wines is made from grapes sourced on the Sonoma Coast (most wines from $22–55). The total annual production is around 7,500 cases. The tasting fee is $15.

# MCKENZIE-MUELLER

2530 Las Amigas Road ✦ Napa
From Carneros/Sonoma Highway (Highway 12/121)
south on Duhig Road *to* Las Amigas Road
*Tel:* 707.252.0186 ✦ www.mckenziemueller.com
Tasting by appointment only

**T**HERE ARE FEW PLACES IN THE WINE COUNTRY WHERE YOU'LL FEEL MORE AT HOME THAN IN THE BARN-STYLE tasting room at McKenzie-Mueller. This working winery and ranch is tucked away on a residential back road where it's easy to forget, even at the height of the summer tourist season when more than five million visitors make their way to Napa's wine country every year. There's none of the glitz and hustle up here— just vineyards and farms and maybe a bit of a breeze coming in off San Pablo Bay.

And, of course, there are friendly folks and some new wines to discover. For a small family operation, making just 3,000 cases of wine a year, McKenzie-Mueller produces an impressive range. Son Julius likes to joke that his parents are so committed to trying a little bit of everything that he even has two middle names. If you're on the tasting trail with someone who can't quite decide on a favorite style, here's the chance to do some serious sampling: you'll find everything from sauvignon blanc and chardonnay to merlot, cabernet franc, cabernet sauvignon, and malbec (most wines $20–45). And, of course, they serve up the Carneros signature wines—beautiful pinot noirs, including a 100% pinot noir rosé that might just be the perfect thing for a summer afternoon in a shady hammock.

The McKenzie and Mueller families have roots here that go back generations. Bob's family settled Napa in the late 1800s and owned vineyards up in Rutherford, but he likes to say that he really learned the craft during his fifteen-year stint as a winemaker over at the University of Mondavi—an affectionate local reference to the generous professional development and entrepreneurial encouragement that Robert Mondavi offered his employees.

Karen and Bob purchased their first ten acres of vineyards in the late 1970s, and a decade later they bought their current property on Las Amigas Road. By the early 1990s, they went into winemaking on their own, full time. All the wines at McKenzie-Mueller are made from estate fruit and are bottled unfiltered. Although these are wines that have won a raft of gold and double gold medals from wine competitions, the emphasis here is on learning to trust your own palate and on finding a wine you'll enjoy. Bob insists that everyone who tastes wine has the ability to make smart judgments, and there's always a standing invitation to come out to their tasting room and give it a try. The $10 tasting fee is waived with purchase, unless you are coming as part of a large group.

# ADASTRA VINEYARDS

2545 Las Amigas Road ✦ Napa
From Carneros/Sonoma Highway (Highway 12/121)
south on Duhig Road *to* Las Amigas Road
*Tel:* 707.255.4818 ✦ www.adastrawines.com
Tasting by appointment only

CHRIS AND NAOMI THORPE BOUGHT THIS THIRTY-THREE-ACRE RANCH IN THE CARNEROS BACK IN THE 1980s, AND their first thought was to raise cattle. But the cattle kept wandering, and Chris likes to joke that he blames his neighbor for getting him into the wine business. The neighbor was clearing his property to put in vineyards and offered to let him use the machinery. So in 1990, the family planted their first eight acres, and later another twelve. Today the vineyards are planted to chardonnay, merlot, pinot noir, and syrah along the northeast slopes, and the family has returned this pre-Prohibition estate to vineyards for the first time in generations.

Known to settlers in the nineteenth century as Rancho Huichica—which translates from the hybridization of Spanish and native Wappo languages as "Owl Ranch"—this property has a long history in the wine country. A Danish family were the first white settlers here in the early 1800s, when they acquired forty acres for a thousand dollars in gold coins as part of a Mexican land grant. The historic ranch still has an old pioneer-style outhouse down at the far end of the lawn. During a recent renovation, Chris discovered an old root and wine cellar under the floorboards in the old farmhouse—complete with hundred-year-old empty

beer bottles. Owls still live in the nineteenth-century barn that serves as the Adastra tasting room.

Chris is an astronomy enthusiast, and the name Adastra comes from the Latin motto *per aspera ad astra*—"through hard work to the stars." Part of that work, of course, is running the winery, which produces fewer than 1,500 cases of 100% estate wines (most $40–60). All the grapes are grown organically. Situated just a few miles from the San Pablo Bay, the vineyards are perfect for cooler climate grapes like pinot noir and chardonnay. The 2005 syrah was awarded an impressive 93 points by *Wine Spectator*. To the delight of gourmet cooks and business travelers, half bottles of Adastra's wines are readily available. Son-in-law Edwin has recently started making around 700 cases a year of California table wine under a second label—Ed's Red ($15; www.edsred.net).

Tasting with the winegrower includes a tour of the historic property. The tasting fee is $20, waived with the purchase of a half case of wine.

# TRUCHARD VINEYARDS

3234 Old Sonoma Road ✦ Napa

Call for directions

*Tel:* 707.253.7153 ✦ www.truchardvineyards.com

Tasting by appointment only, closed Sunday

S OMETIMES LIFE IN THE WINE COUNTRY BEGINS IN THE MOST UNUSUAL WAY, AND, IF YOU START ASKING THE county's winemakers how they got their start, you'll hear stories of honeymoon weekends or lucky invitations or chance encounters. But the story that Jo Ann and Tony Truchard tell might just be the most fateful of all, because, as they will tell you, it all began with Jo Ann slipping on a grape in 1972.

Back then, Tony was an Army doctor who had just received orders

to Korea when his wife slipped on a grape in the local grocery store and broke her knee. Four days later, the couple's son was born, and, instead of going to Korea, the family ended up on the Army base in Herlong, California.

That autumn, they visited Napa. Tony had grown up on a ranch in Texas, where his French grandfather had planted a small vineyard in the Lone Star State for years. Enchanted by Napa, they started looking for a piece of property and ended up finding the perfect spot—a twenty-one-acre parcel in the Carneros region, planted to pastures and prune orchards, which they visited on weekends. They converted the property to vineyards and sold their grapes to the Carneros Creek Winery. Then, in 1987, Tony bought a local medical practice, and the couple moved to Napa full time. Two years later, Truchard Vineyards released its first commercial vintage, specializing in pinot noir and chardonnay—the signature varietals of this southern sub-appellation.

Today, the couple farms around 270 acres of their 400-acre property, making around a dozen different wines from ten different varietals (from $20–75, most around $35). By Napa Valley standards, this is a huge piece of property, but, as they will tell you, they are a large vineyard and a small winery—producing around 17,000 cases of wine and selling the majority of their fruit to other winemakers in the region.

While they still make some of the signature Carneros pinot noir and chardonnay, Truchard also produces excellent cabernet sauvignon, petit verdot, cabernet franc, and merlot wines. As one of the warmest vineyards in the appellation, they are able to get great fruit from some of the traditional Bordeaux varietals—and from spicier fruits like syrah, zinfandel, and tempranillo. In addition to the chardonnay, there is also a small roussanne program. The *San Francisco Chronicle* named the winery's 2006 roussanne one of the top 100 wines of the year—and at $20

a bottle, it's one of the valley's best deals. You'll also find a late-harvest dessert, wine made from roussanne, and if you aren't familiar with either this Rhône varietal or with the magic of botrytis, the noble rot, Truchard is a great place to discover something new.

All the wines are 100% estate, with the emphasis on wines crafted without a lot of manipulation that age well and are easy to enjoy with food. Tastings take place in a rustic redwood barn next door to the family's farmhouse, and the visit includes a tour of the caves. The path up to the vineyards is lined with roses that come tumbling out in all directions. Here at Truchard, where there are so many different varietals on the property, the harvest goes on sometimes as long as ten weeks, and the fruit is still hand-harvested. You are welcome to come for a visit during the crush. There is no charge for a tasting unless you are part of a large group.

# JONESY'S FAMOUS STEAK HOUSE

2044 Airport Road ✦ Napa

*Tel.* 707.255.2003 ✦ www.jonesysfamoussteakhouse.com

Sunday *to* Thursday 10AM *to* 8PM, Friday and Saturday until 9PM

OST VISITORS TO THE NAPA VALLEY NEVER DISCOVER ONE OF THE AREA'S BEST STEAKHOUSES BECAUSE IT'S tucked away just beyond the terminals at the Napa Regional Airport, where the rich and famous arrive by private jet for their wine-tasting weekends. You may come across them at Jonesy's Famous Steak House, but it is also where local families come to celebrate special occasions, and happy hour in the bar is a favorite spot for socializing and watching sunsets over the valley.

Here, the steaks are hand carved and grilled under local river rocks, and you can settle back with an old-style cocktail to watch the world come and go. There is a good local wine list, but the real bargain is the corkage ($7.50). Here's the perfect opportunity to open one of those bottles that you've picked up along the way and discover new ways to pair Napa's famous hillside cabernets with gourmet cooking. Most entrees are priced around $20.

# WINE SHIPPING SERVICES

UPS STORE

1436 Second Street ✦ Napa ✦ Downtown Napa

*Tel* 707.265.6011 ✦ www.theupsstore.com

Monday to Friday 8:30AM *to* 6:30PM, Saturday 9AM *to* 5PM

THIS LITTLE OUTLET IN DOWNTOWN NAPA SPECIALIZES IN HELPING VISITORS GET THEIR WINES HOME SAFELY AND economically, and I know of more than a few small wineries who use their services. The last time I needed to get a case of wine to New England, the young woman behind the counter kindly helped me figure out how to fit all those oddly shaped bottles of sparkling wine into the sturdy cardboard boxes that they provide, taped it up for me, and, for less than $80—a price that included the shipping and packaging—dispatched my precious cargo on its way east. The services are well priced and convenient, while the staff is friendly.

NAPA VALLEY WINE STORAGE

1135 Golden Gate Drive ✦ Napa

From St. Helena Highway (Highway 29) exit

West Imola Avenue west *to* Golden Gate Drive south

*Tel* 707.265.9990 ✦ www.napavalleywinestorage.com

MANY OF THE WINE COUNTRY'S MOST SERIOUS COLLECTORS RELY ON NAPA VALLEY WINE STORAGE, which offers high end temperature- and humidity-controlled storage facilities. They also offer a range of shipping services. They will pick up from local wineries in both Napa and Sonoma counties, or you can arrange to drop off cases before heading out of town. If you're ending your tasting adventures along the Highway 12/121, en route back to the Oakland or San Francisco airports, Napa is an easy stop.

STAGE COACH EXPRESS AND COMPANY
3379 Solano Avenue ✦ Napa
Solano Avenue just south of Redwood Road/Trancas Street
*Tel:* 707.257.1888 ✦ www.stagecoachexpress.com

ONE OF THE FAVORITE SHIPPING COMPANIES AMONG THE SMALL FAMILY VINTNERS, STAGE COACH EXPRESS CAN help find a way to get your new collection back home, often even if you live in a state where bottles can't be shipped directly from the winery. Proprietors Sue Bailey and Larry Rupp can arrange to pick up wines from local hotels or from the wineries, which is especially handy if you are thinking of joining wine clubs or buying futures to take advantage of the often significant discounts. Keep in mind that the company doesn't insure for temperature damage, so spring and autumn wine-tasting trips are often more economical times of the year for shipping as well. Prices for delivering a case of wine start at around $70.

# INDEX

## ABOUT THE AUTHOR

〜✺〜

TILAR J. MAZZEO IS THE AUTHOR OF the New York Times best selling biography *The Widow Clicquot* and the forthcoming *Secret of Chanel No. 5* (both HarperCollins), as well as *Back-Lane Wineries of Sonoma* (The Little Bookroom). A professor of English at Colby College, in Waterville, Maine, she lives and works in coastal Maine, Sonoma County, California, and New York City.

## ABOUT THE PHOTOGRAPHER

〜✺〜

RAISED ON HIS FAMILY'S VINEYARD overlooking the Dry Creek Valley, Paul Hawley is a wine country native. He graduated from the University of California Santa Cruz in 2003 with a degree in film production. You can find him most days in the cellar at Hawley Winery or behind his lens somewhere along the beautiful back roads of Sonoma County and beyond. Photography and filmmaking remain a passion, and Paul's feature film, *Corked*, premiered at film festivals in 2008.